Concise Catholic Dictionary

Reynolds R. Ekstrom
Rosemary Ekstrom

TWENTY-THIRD PUBLICATIONS
P.O. Box 180 • Mystic, CT 06355

Fourth printing 1986
Third printing 1985
Second printing 1983
First printing 1982

Edited by Gwen Costello
Designed by John G. van Bemmel
Cover by Robert Maitland

ISBN 0-89622-159-8
Library of Congress Catalog Card Number 82-82386

"...just the tool parish directors have been looking for to help parents understand how concepts are taught today in their children's religion classes."

"Its main value will lie in its availability for the informal and haphazard discussions that arise at the dinner table, at parties, in bars, barbershops, or prayer meetings. It may well serve to bring these meandering 'Well, I think,' and 'I was always taught' interchanges to a factual, balanced, informed, regrouping point."

"This may be what you've been looking for to bolster catechist knowledge and confidence."

"This work will be welcomed by many."

LIST OF ARTICLES

(See Index starting on page 165 for fuller listing of terms of interest incorporated within the major entries).

ACKNOWLEDGMENTS

We acknowledge our great debt and our deep gratitude to all who have assisted us in the development of this work. We wish especially and sincerely to thank the following people for their thorough critiques and timely recommendations:

Rev. Johannes Hofinger, S.J., Director of the Pontifical Institute of Catechetics & Spirituality, New Orleans; also Associate Director of Religious Education, Archdiocese of New Orleans.

Rev. Gerald M. Fagin, S.J., Director of the Graduate Religious Studies Department, Loyola Univeristy of the South, New Orleans.

Rev. Maurice Monette, O.M.I., Former Director of the Catechetical & Pastoral Institute of Loyola (Graduate Program), Loyola University, New Orleans.

Dominick Gulotta, Religion Department Chairman, Holy Cross High School, New Orleans; also Theology and Catechetics Instructor, St. Mary's Dominican College, New Orleans.

In addition, we acknowledge and thank the following persons for their gracious commitment of time and supportive energies: Deacon Paul Nalty, a fine friend and wise attorney, one who is always prepared to serve when called upon; Rev. George Fitzgerald, C.S.P., who planted the seed of a good idea; Rev. Paul Calamari, Director of the Office of Religious Education, New Orleans, for his support and gentle encouragement; Mrs. Marion Gourgues, for all of her secretarial assistance; and William Holub and John van Bemmel of Twenty-Third Publications for their needed direction and invaluable advice.

INTRODUCTION

The idea for this book was first formed almost a decade ago. Over the years, in our various catechetical ministries, we have heard learners and co-workers question what it means to be Catholic today. They have asked (and we have too, of course), what is so unique, important, and distinctive about being a Catholic Christian. They have wondered how Catholic beliefs and practices differ from those of other Christian religions. Quite simply, they have not been sure which beliefs, attitudes, and practices to hand on to coming generations. They have not known how to explain the Catholic faith to others adequately and confidently.

In recent decades Catholics have become more aware of their identity as Christians, but they haven't always understood what is unique about being *Catholic* Christians. They want to understand, appreciate, and hand on the special teachings, values, and practices of their Catholic community.

This dictionary is our effort to introduce or reintroduce the many teachings, facts, beliefs, and values that are special and basic to the Catholic community. Of course, we haven't covered everything about Catholicism. We had to be selective because of space limitations. We have included hundreds of topics because the scope of our study, Catholicism, is enormous. Yet we wanted to offer Catholics and inquirers into Catholicism a book that would answer many of their questions, but that would also be most convenient to use.

Three features are included in this book to maximize its usefulness.

The list of articles at the front of this book has two kinds of entries. Some are listed with a page number indicating where the article begins. Other entries are followed by a cross reference; for example: Blessed Sacrament (see Eucharist, Tabernacle). Words listed in this way guide the reader to major terms that appear under a different title.

A second kind of cross reference is used in the body of the book. At the end of each article the reader is referred to other articles for more information on the same subject. For example, at the end of Confirmation, it is suggested: See also Anointing, Catechumenate and the RCIA, Sacraments.

Finally, there is an exhaustive index at the end of the book, directing the reader to any of several hundred terms that may be of interest.

To achieve brevity and clarity, but also to avoid over-simplification, we will use the following four-step process to explain most of the topics:

Step 1 In the first paragraph we will provide (as far as possible) a clear and concise *definition* of the topic under consideration.

Step 2 In the second paragraph we will offer some *historical data* about the topic. We will try to show how the Catholic community's understanding and appreciation of it has developed over the centuries.

Step 3 In the third paragraph we will introduce, where possible, some *recent theological thinking* about the topic.

Step 4 In the fourth paragraph we will normally emphasize *current official statements* of the Catholic Church about the topic.

Because our treatment of these topics is brief, we hope our readers will want to do some follow-up, in-depth study. To assist them in this, we have included a select bibliography at the end of our text. It lists recent books that will help them investigate individual topics more thoroughly.

A marvelous, living tradition has been handed on to Catholics over the centuries. Many contemporary Catholics and those who wish to become Catholic yearn to fully investigate, appreciate, and understand this ongoing, unique tradition. They also seek to hand on this tradition faithfully and carefully to children in their homes and to students in their classes. If this dictionary helps them in some small way to do this, we will be most content.

AARON   a Hebrew figure from Old Testament times, was the brother of Moses and the son of Amran and Jochebed. According to longstanding biblical and Jewish tradition, Aaron was the high priest of the Hebrews who were the "chosen people" of Yahweh (God). The exact meaning of the name Aaron is not known.

Aaron acted as a spokesman for Moses before Egypt's pharaoh. Moses apparently had a speech problem and was very reluctant to speak for himself. Aaron also had a role in the plague stories, and he made a trip to the top of Mt. Sinai with Moses on at least one occasion. He assisted the "praying" Moses in a crucial battle against an enemy army. In the book of Numbers it is recorded that Aaron (like Moses) died before his people reached the promised land of Canaan. It is believed that he was buried on Mount Hor near the land of Edom. Before his death the "garments" of the high priest, Aaron, were taken from him and passed on to Eleazar his son. (Deuteronomy reports that Aaron's death and burial, plus the passing of his priestly office to Eleazar, occurred at a place called Moserah.)

In Saint Paul's Epistle to the Hebrews in the New Testament, the old covenant priesthood is contrasted with Jesus Christ's perfected priesthood of the new covenant (Heb 7:11-28). Bible scholars suspect that the many elaborations and the many years of Hebrew oral tradition have obscured the actual historical character of Moses' brother, Aaron.

Note of interest: It seems Aaron was capable of remarkable failings. His early death, prior to entry into the Promised Land, was very likely a punishment for some sin (lack of faith in Yahweh?). Whatever it was happened before the water miracle at Meribah-Kadesh (Nm 20:2-13). Recall also the golden calf story (Ex 32), in which Aaron, watching over the people in Moses' absence, was pressured by his contemporaries to perform foolish and idolatrous actions. (See also Hebrews, Moses, Passover.)

ABORTION   is any procedure that deliberately removes a fetus from the mother's womb before he or she is capable of independent life. The Catholic Church teaches that an embryo or fetus is actually a living human being, and therefore no other human being has the right to terminate this life. In the United States, and in many other countries, abortions are allowed by law. Nevertheless the church teaches that abortion is wrong because it takes away a defenseless human being's right to life. Many Catholics today belong to the "Right to Life" movement, a pro-life, anti-abortion movement.

Abortions were performed quite often during the first century after Christ, and early Christians were taught that they must never seek abortions. At least one early church document called abortion an act of murder. Several church leaders—including Clement of Alexandria, Saint Jerome, and Saint Augustine—firmly taught that abortion is an evil practice. During the 4th century, the Church of Spain decreed that persons who committed the sin of abortion could never again receive communion. Many of the church's popes and great teachers have likewise condemned abortion over the centuries.

In more recent times, Pope John XXIII and Vatican Council II have noted the evil effects of legalized abortions on the whole of society. Numerous church leaders affirm that human life does indeed begin at the very moment of conception. Therefore "direct abortion" (the deliberate removal of a fetus from a woman's body), causes the unnecessary death of a fully human individual.

According to Catholic teaching, abortion violates the 5th Commandment. Women who have abortions, as well as those who perform them, are excommunicated from the church. American bishops have declared that abortion is a sin against the weak and the helpless and that all Catholics should work hard to stop abortions from taking place. The bishops have also noted that women who seek abortions need and deserve the constant help of all Catholics as they try to find solutions to their problems.

Note of Interest: In the United States abortion on demand during the first six months of pregnancy was legalized by the Supreme Court decision, *Wade vs. Roe*, on January 22, 1973. (See also Commandments of God, Sin.)

ABRAHAM   was the first of the great ancestors and founders of the Hebrew people. Christians and Jews alike honor Abraham for his great faith and complete trust in God.

The bible reports that Abraham was the husband of Sarah and the father of Isaac. He lived about 1800 years before Christ and was the leader of a tribe (or clan) of people. Abraham received and answered a special call from God and faithfully moved his family, his clansmen, and his possessions from the city of Haran to the land called Canaan.

Such moves by tribes or clans were fairly common during Abraham's time. Yet his story is important to all Christians for four reasons: 1) God chose to reveal himself to Abraham, 2) Abraham was the first person to wholly trust and believe in the one, true God, 3) He believed in a personal friendship between the one God and humankind, 4) God loved Abraham so much that he made a covenant with him, promising Abraham a beautiful new homeland and countless blessings on his numerous descendants if they had faith and served God.

Catholics revere Abraham as one of the great fathers of the Hebrew people, the nation of Israel, and the chosen people of God. From this nation came Jesus Christ, the messiah, founder of the church and the "new people of God". Catholics look upon Abraham as a model of faith and trust in God. (See also Bible, Covenant, Old Testament.)

ACTS OF THE APOSTLES is that book in the New Testament that immediately follows the four gospels. The author of the gospel of Luke wrote Acts, about the year A.D. 80, so that he could tell of some outstanding events and happenings in the early days of the Christian community. The book, Acts of the Apostles, was never intended to be a complete history of the early church.

The early Greek name of this book was *Praxeis Apostolon*, "acts of apostles." Thus the current title, Acts of the Apostles, is not quite accurate, since the book does indeed tell of much more than simply the works of the original apostles of the Lord Jesus.

The first major portion of the book centers on Saint Peter, the first pope of the church community. The second portion centers on the missionary and evangelizing work of Saint Paul and his companions. The real "turning point" in the Acts of the Apostles comes with the rather long report on the Council of Jerusalem. After that meeting of church community leaders, Christianity turned its focus away from Jerusalem and the strict law of the Jewish faith, and began preaching and teaching the gospel of the risen Jesus in the city of Rome and in many nations around the known world.

Very likely Luke was a preacher who traveled with Saint Paul. Catholic Christians view Acts of the Apostles as an inspired work that shows how the "good news" of Jesus was spread throughout the whole earth. The author of this book also wanted to stress that it is the Spirit of the Lord—the same Spirit sent by the risen Jesus to his followers—who guides the present life of the church, the Body of Christ. (See also Bible, New Testament.)

ACTUAL SIN   is any willful thought, action, or failure-to-act that either weakens or causes a total break in our loving relationship with God. The sin that weakens this relationship has traditionally been called venial sin. Serious sin that causes a complete break with God is called mortal sin or deadly sin. Actual sin differs from original sin in that we humans are "actually" responsible for these sins, whereas original sin is that sinful state of the world into which we are born.

The Catholic Church teaches that actual sin, whether serious or not-so-serious, can be forgiven by God when sinners are truly sorry and desire to sin no more. People often seek to renew their loving relationships with God after they have committed sin and so the church offers opportunities to do so in the sacrament of reconciliation.

The church also provides certain times (such as the seasons of Advent and Lent) and special, prayerful devotions (like parish renewals) to help Catholics repent and make reparation for their sins. (See also Reconciliation, Sin.)

ADAM and EVE   are the symbolic names given in the Book of Genesis to the "first" man and woman of the human race. The word Adam has Hebrew origins which mean simply "the man." It is also a play on the Hebrew word for "dust" or "ground." The word Eve, which means "the living one," also has Hebrew roots. The bible says that Adam and Eve were the parents of three sons: Cain, Abel, and Seth.

There are two distinct accounts of creation in Genesis (1:26, 2:3, and 2:4–25). Using highly poetic and symbolic imagery, the author of Genesis says that God created the man from the dust of the earth and breathed life into him. Then God made Eve from one of Adam's ribs. The two enjoyed life in Paradise until they fell into sinfulness and suffered its terrible effects. Before they sinned, Adam and Eve enjoyed an intimate friendship with God and possessed God's grace and other gifts. Saint Paul compared Jesus with Adam, saying that Jesus is a "new Adam" through whom comes eternal life and salvation from sin and evil. A number of great church thinkers, for example, Augustine, Irenaeus, and Thomas Aquinas, have compared Eve with Mary, the mother of Christ. Through Eve disobedience and sin entered the world, whereas through Mary's loving obedience to God, life and redemption have been made possible for humankind. Significant statements about the creation humankind were made by the 4th Lateran Council (1215), by Vatican I (1870), and by Pope Pius XII in his encyclical, *Humani Generis*, in 1950.

During the 20th century there has been some debate among Catholics as to whether there was only one set of parents for the entire human race (mongenism), or more than one original set of human ancestors (polygenism). The ordinary magisterium of the church teaches that humans come from a single pair of human beings. Paul VI declared in 1966 that the theory of polygenism has not yet been proved by modern science and must be avoided if it will lead to the denial of the church's doctrine on original sin. There may very well have been more than one original set of human parents, but this does not necessarily conflict with traditional teachings on original sin. Further scientific studies will likely establish whether polygenist or monogenist ideas are more correct.

The church emphasizes that God the creator freely and immediately created the human soul, giving human beings grace and friendship. God created humans in his own image and then placed them at the highest level of created order. Through their sin the first persons, Adam and Eve, lost God's great friendship and the paradise they enjoyed. The effects of this sin of Adam (called original sin) is inherited by all humans at the time of birth. The church likewise teaches that humans were meant by God to be happy, that they have a special duty to care for the world. Adam is the "father" of all human beings and Jesus, the "new Adam," provides the human race with salvation from sin and the promise of eternal happiness. (See also Creation, Old Testament.)

ADVENT is the season of the church year that begins on the first Sunday after the feast of Saint Andrew, which is on November 30th. The word *advent* comes from the term *adventus* which means coming. During this season Catholics celebrate the coming of the Lord Jesus to earth, and his continuing presence in the church community. They prepare for his return in glory in the future through on-going conversion. The bible readings of the advent liturgies help Catholics understand the meaning of Christ's life on earth as well as his presence in the church to this day.

The advent season was celebrated by Christians in some parts of Europe before 500 A.D., but not by the entire Roman Catholic Church until the 6th century. By the 8th century the first Sunday of advent marked the beginning of the official church year. During the 9th century Pope Gregory I shortened the advent season from six weeks to four weeks. He also wrote many prayers and chose bible readings for the Advent liturgies.

To this day Catholics celebrate Advent in order to become more aware of Jesus Christ's continuing presence in the church and to think about the fact that he became man in order to save the human race from sinfulness. The scripture readings for the first two weeks of the season focus on Jesus' coming at the world's end to judge all men and women. The readings for the second half of Advent center on the special joy and hope of the Christmas feast. The liturgical colors of the season are purple and rose, signifying *metanoia* (change) and hope. Each Advent season is a special time for every believer to open his/her heart more fully to the love of God and to the eternal salvation offered to all by Jesus Christ the savior. (See also Christmas, Conversion, Liturgical year.)

ALL SAINTS DAY   is a Catholic holy day of obligation that is celebrated on November 1st, and is the feast day on which we honor all saints who are enjoying life in heaven—especially those saints who do not have feast days on the official church calendar.

Christians were setting aside May 13th to honor all martyrs as early as the 4th century. In the year 609, Pope Boniface IV was able to make a pagan temple in Rome—the Pantheon—a Christian church. He chose to do this on May 13th and dedicated this happy event and the new church to Mary and to all Christian martyrs. Pope Gregory III changed the date of this feast to November 1st in 732, and by the 12th century all Catholics were accepting November 1st as the official All Saints' Day.

The vigil (a night of prayerful waiting for a feast) and the octave (a joyful eight-day period after a feast) were once observed for All Saints' Day, but have not been observed by Catholics since 1955. However, the church still teaches that everyone in heaven is a saint, that this feast day is a special time to pray to saints for help with our troubles, and as Pope Paul VI said in 1977: We honor those who have left us a heritage of examples, a true school of human and Christian virtue. (See also Canonization; Heaven; Saints, Communion of.)

ALL SOULS DAY   is a day set aside by the church, usually November 2nd, on which we recall and pray for the dead who are in purgatory. The feast was established by Saint Odilo in the 10th century so that monks in his abbey could offer special prayers and songs for the dead on the day after All Saints Day, November 1st.

This practice became popular and spread to many Catholic communities in Europe and Latin America. During the 15th century, some priests began offering three Masses on All Souls Day. This custom was made a formal church practice, *circa* 1920, when Pope Benedict XV allowed priests to say three Masses on November 2nd: one to be offered for a special intention, one for the dead in purgatory, and one for the pope's intentions.

The reasons for many of the prayers and Masses on November 2nd in the distant past were fear and superstition. For example some people thought that the souls of the dead would really appear to them. The custom of offering three Masses is still practiced by some priests to this day. The church provides a guide, Masses For the Dead, from which readings may be chosen for these Masses. Vestments for the day are black or purple—but local church custom allows for other colors as well.

Catholic thinking about this feast centers on the fact that even though people have died and gone into the condition (or state) we call purgatory, they will proceed from this time of being-made-pure to the happiness of heaven. These souls need the prayers of Christian believers, especially the Eucharist, because they are not able to help themselves get to heaven once they are in purgatory. (See also Heaven, Purgatory.)

ANNULMENT is an official decision on the part of the church that a marriage was invalid from its very beginning and, therefore, never really existed. This decision is usually made by a diocesan marriage tribunal or by some other church authority, such as the local bishop. A more accurate term for the annulment decision is a decree of nullity.

There are a number of reasons why annulments can be granted to Catholics. For instance, if marriage partners never intended to have children or they did not intend to make their relationship permanent, an annulment can be granted. If a Catholic is married to another by a non-Catholic minister without special permission, if a man and woman have married but have never had sexual intercourse, or if one of them had never recieved Christian baptism by the time of marriage, the church often gives an annulment.

In recent years, the Catholic Church has been very active in making "decrees of nullity." To be validly married persons must enter the marriage covenant freely and with full understanding of what they are doing. The church recognizes that pressures placed on men and women by modern life make true and lasting commitments more and more difficult.

However the church's marriage courts are not making it easier for persons to gain "decrees of nullity" these days. It is just that marriage tribunals recognize that in some cases—for a number of understandable reasons—couples have never been able to live a sacramental, covenant relationship.

Note of Interest: In January 1981 John Paul II noted the "alarming increase in marriage cases in church courts" and held that too-easily obtained decrees of nullity could negatively influence preparation for matrimony. He has called, also, for a full review of current annulment policy. (See also Divorce, Matrimony.)

ANOINTING   is the act of pouring or rubbing special oil on a person or thing in order to make the "anointed" sacred and consecrated to God.

During Old Testament times, olive oil was used for medical purposes, as fuel, for bathing, and for anointing in sacred ceremonies. In ancient Israel anointing was done to refresh and strengthen a person and to bring God's Spirit upon him/her when an important mission was to be undertaken. Prophets and priests were the ones who did this holy anointing. Israelite Kings Saul, David, and Solomon were all anointed.

Jesus the Messiah, was sent by God to save humankind from sin. The word Christ is derived from the Greek term for "the anointed." Jesus healed many people who were suffering through sickness and other ills. It is reported in the gospels and in the Acts of the Apostles that the earliest followers of Jesus also healed many sick people and, in some cases, anointed them, The Epistle of James (5:14–15) notes that anointing sick people with oil, in the name of the risen Jesus Christ, will help strengthen and heal them.

The church continues to anoint individuals in the sacraments of baptism, confirmation, holy orders, and anointing of the sick. It believes that anointing with oil makes them more holy, strengthened and freshened, and better able to endure hardships such as pain, fears, tension, and discouragement. The holy chrism (the oil), used in anointing ceremonies is blessed by Catholic bishops on Holy Thursday. (See also Anointing of the Sick, Baptism, Confirmation.)

ANOINTING OF THE SICK   is one of the seven sacraments of the Catholic faith. It is given to persons who are very sick or weakened by illness, and to persons who are in danger of death. A priest or deacon anoints these individuals by putting holy oil on their hands and foreheads while saying, "May the Lord who frees you from sin save you and raise you up." After the anointing the minister says: "Lord Jesus Christ, you shared in our human nature to heal the sick and save all mankind."

In 9th century Europe it was a church custom that the sick and dying be anointed in a "sacrament of the sick." By the 12th century this sacrament was viewed as a last anointing before passage to eternal life. By the 16th century, the time of the Council of Trent, the sacrament was called extreme unction. The church ordered, in very recent times, that the name of the sacrament be anointing of the sick. It called for significant revisions in the rituals for offering the sacrament to Catholics. Official changes in the anointing rituals were issued by the Vatican on January 18, 1973.

Anointing of the sick can now be celebrated within the Mass in order that the prayers of the entire congregation might be offered on behalf of the sick and dying. When the sacrament is celebrated outside of Mass, the persons being anointed first confess their sins to a priest, are then anointed with oil, and receive *Viaticum* (holy communion). In this ceremony the minister who does the anointing represents the church community, which hopes and prays that the ill persons will be made stronger and regain health. Through this sacrament the whole church prays that the risen Christ will grant "relief and salvation" to those who are anointed.

The church teaches that the anointing of the sick makes persons stronger in body and spirit and that it may forgive actual sin, and take away some of the "temporal punishment" (in purgatory) due for sins already forgiven. This sacrament is a sign of Jesus Christ's great love and concern for the bodily and spiritual health of members of the church community. It also recalls that Christ suffered much for humanity. One need not be in immediate danger of death in order to receive the anointing of the sick. The biblical passage most often cited to show that even the earliest Christians anointed the sick and suffering members of the community is James 5:14–15.

In the church document, *Rite Of Anointing And Pastoral Care of the Sick*, published by the Vatican in the 1970s, it is stated that the following may receive the sacrament: 1) Those dangerously ill due to sickness or old age. 2) Older persons—if they are in a weakened condition, even though no dangerous illness is present. 3) Sick children and youth, if they have "sufficient use of reason to be comforted by this sacrament." 4) Individuals who have recovered from an illness after being anointed. 5) Individuals who have been anointed during an illness may receive this sacrament again if the "danger becomes more serious." 6) A sick person "should be anointed before surgery" whenever a dangerous illness is involved. 7) Persons who lose consciousness or the use of reason may be anointed if—as faithful Christians—they would have sought the sacrament "if they were in control of their faculties." *Note of Interest*: Priests are not permitted to anoint the body of an individual who has already died. If there is any doubt whether the person has or has not died, the sacrament may be administered conditionally. (See also Anointing, Sacraments.)

APOCALYPSE known today as the book of Revelation is the title of the last book of the New Testament. The word Apocalypse, derived from the Greek, means revealed. The Apocalypse centers on certain visions of a man named John of Patmos. The visions are about events to come in the future, and include warnings about the worldly evils faced by early Christians. The book was probably completed about 95 A.D. and is the work of several editors/authors.

Some church leaders at first rejected the Apocalypse, but later agreed that it should, indeed, be part of sacred scripture. The text of the Apocalypse, using the Old Testament as a basic resource, tells of a crisis-time during the earliest days of Christianity and how the forces of goodness must struggle with the forces of evil.

The literary form of the book of Revelation must be considered in order to accurately interpret and understand it. This book is a narrative (and allegory) in which the prophet John receives revelations from Jesus Christ (the "visions"), and he proceeds to describe his visions using rich imagery. The revelations and visions center on a situation of conflict and persecution suffered by John's Christian contemporaries who were being persecuted by the Romans. The Roman Emperor is described as an Antichrist. Modern biblical critics generally hold that the original hearers/readers of Revelation understood that this corrupted world must be destroyed before the kingdom promised by Jesus could truly reign. Therefore reality is described as a continuing struggle by the powers of the good against evil and death. Physical death is not a finality, not some useless bitter end, but part of a process. Just as Jesus endured powerlessness, pain, and death, so must his followers in times of persecution. Just as Jesus is risen from death, so will his faithful followers enjoy eternal light and life and happiness in the heavenly kingdom. In this world the followers of Christ must endure hardship as they strive for justice, peace, and holiness.

The author, or authors, of the Apocalypse are not precisely known. John the Evangelist was probably not the author, nor were the writers/editors of the johannine letters or Saint John's Gospel. At any rate the book of Revelation is not to be used as a tool for predicting or revealing the end of the world. Much more research is needed in order that Catholics and others will fully grasp the meaning(s) and purpose(s) of Revelation for early Christians and for present-day Catholics. (See also Bible, New Testament.)

APOSTLES were the twelve men chosen by Jesus Christ to hear and believe in the good news of salvation that he proclaimed.

After the resurrection they were commissioned to preach and teach the good news and to baptize persons all over the world in Jesus' name.

The list of the original apostles appears in the gospels of Mark, Matthew, and Luke, and in the Acts of the Apostles. The names of the 12 apostles were Simon Peter, Matthew, James the Greater, James the Less, John, Judas, Andrew, Philip, Bartholomew (also called Nathaniel), Thomas, Thaddeus (also known as Jude), and Simon the Zealot. After the death of Judas, the apostle who betrayed Jesus, Matthias was chosen to replace him. Saint Paul is often referred to as an apostle but he was not one of the original twelve.

In the Old Testament, the nation of Israel (the people of God), was made up of twelve tribes, which were led by the 12 sons of Jacob. In the New Testament Jesus gives the 12 apostles responsibility to lead the church (the new Israel, and the new People of God), and to guide all believers. The apostles preached and taught the gospel message, worshipped God the Father with other faithful believers, and continued to act in the name of Jesus the Lord.

The apostle Peter was the church's first pope. The popes who have followed him are his direct successors. The apostles are considered the first bishops. When a man becomes a bishop of the church he is a true successor of the original twelve.

Note of Interest: A recent statement by a team of biblical scholars, drawn together in the late 1970s by the Catholic Biblical Association of America (to look into the overall New Testament evidence on women and priestly ministry), concluded that the "circle of twelve is the only exclusively male group associated with Jesus." These men came from a wider circle of disciples (those who heard Jesus' call and freely chose to follow him), which was not restricted to males (see Mk 15:40-41 and Lk 8:1-3). While the heralded twelve were apostles, the actual circle of them was wider too, including, among others, Paul and Barnabas. Some writers have suggested that there were women apostles, for example, Mary of Magdala, a woman named Junia who is mentioned in Rom 16:7, and Phoebe, who appears in Rom 16:1. New Testament evidence indicates that both men and women were apostles in the primitive church. (See also Acts of the Apostles, Peter.)

ASCENSION THURSDAY   is a special day of the church year on which Catholics celebrate the glorified and victorious return of the risen Jesus to his Father in heaven. The feast occurs on a Thursday, 40 days after Easter. The feast of the Ascension is a holy day in the United States.

Through history the Ascension has commemorated the moment when Christ entered the place of eternal life in order to send the Holy Spirit to his followers. Early Christians considered the Ascension one of the greatest feasts since it is a wonderful sign that all human beings are meant to be united with God in happiness forever.

The gospels of Luke and John seem to indicate that the Ascension happened on Easter night. But the Acts of the Apostles places it some forty days after Easter Sunday. The reason for the Ascension, however, is more crucial than the when of the event. Jesus Christ returned (or rose), to heaven in full glory. Seated at God's right hand, he sent forth his Spirit to his church and to the members of his church in this world. Jesus lived, died, was raised from the dead, and will come again in glory at the end of time.

The Ascension begins the prayerful nine-day wait for the feast of the sending of the Spirit called Pentecost. The risen Jesus is not absent from our world but is present to his followers through the Spirit. The Ascension is a powerful sign of the coming happiness with God in heaven that Jesus promised.

Note of Interest: Biblical accounts of the Ascension of the risen Jesus include Mk 16:19, Lk 24:51, and Acts 1:2. (See also Easter, Heaven, Resurrection.)

ASSUMPTION OF MARY   is celebrated each year by the church on August 15th and is a holyday in the United States. On this day Catholics remember and honor the Blessed Virgin Mary's entry into heaven.

This feast was a popular celebration for Middle East Christians of the 5th century, and it was widespread in Europe some 200 years later. In 1568 Pope Pius V made the Assumption feast a holyday for the entire church. The fact of Mary's assumption was proclaimed a dogma of the Catholic faith by Pope Pius XII, on November 1, 1950, in his statement, *"Munificentissimus Deus."*

Official church teaching on the assumption of Mary states that she went to heaven, body and soul united, but it does not say whether or not she died first. Many early Christians thought Mary was taken into heaven prior to death because she was totally sinless. (See also Dogma, Mary.)

ATHEISM   is a manner of thinking and acting through which a human being denies the reality of God. A contemporary word that describes the attitude of an atheist is unbelief. In recent years the church has stated that atheism is one of the major problems plaguing humankind. The term atheism is derived from the Greek *atheos*, which means "living without a god."

The marked increase in the number of persons who profess atheism (making it, truly, one of the more obvious "signs of our times") can be attributed to the cynicism, the stresses, pressures, and the overt criticisms of religious systems and beliefs that characterize the modern era. These attitudes can be traced back directly to the philosophical works (19th century) of Hegel, Marx, Engels, Comte, Schopenhauer, Nietzsche, and others. Leaders of the church have consistently spoken out against the evils of atheism. In this century five popes have dealt with this problem, including Pope John Paul II. During the mid-1960s, Vatican Council II addressed the matter of modern atheistic behavior in the *Pastoral Constitution On The Church In The Modern World*.

Vatican II acknowledged some forms and causes of atheism that exist today. These include: 1) failure to believe in God because he is a great mystery; 2) over-reliance on scientific method alone; 3) a "humanism" that extols human beings to the exclusion of God; 4) mistaken ideas about God and/or religion; 5) protest against the very existence of evil; 6) lives focused upon gaining pleasures or material goods; and 7) immoral or unworthy example of those who profess belief in God. Two notions fuel atheistic attitudes and lifestyles. The first notion is that faith and dependence on an Other is somehow in contradiction to true human freedom and independence. The second notion is that belief and religious systems are like drugs (opiates) which sedate people and induce them to simply hope for an unreal future existence in a nebulous eternity.

Vatican II presented two "remedies" for atheism: 1) show clearly that Christian faith does not deny human freedom or belittle authentic human rights and dignity; and 2) church members are urged to witness daily to the gospel message, proclaim Christian teachings, and encourage all people of god to participate in works of justice, loving mercy, and forgiveness. The church also recommends "sincere and prudent dialogue" on the gospel, on social and economic problems that thwart human development, and on modern personal pressures. The council also taught that the people of god bear some responsibility for the increase of atheism. When church members willfully neglect their Christian training, teach erroneous doctrine, "or are deficient in their religious, moral, or social life," they are concealing the "authentic face of God and religion."

Note of Interest: An agnostic is different from an atheist. While the latter freely denies the reality of God's existence, an agnostic person holds to the theory that humans cannot scientifically know or discover the immaterial. Thus they cannot know—with certainty—that the spiritual, immaterial, unseen God really exists. The terms agnostic and agnosticism come from the Greek *agnostos*, which means "unknowable." (See also Faith, Monotheism, Trinity.)

BALTIMORE CATECHISM   is a book containing the basic beliefs and teachings of the Catholic faith that has been used in the United States to instruct young people and adults. Teachers who use the Baltimore Catechism impart the doctrines of Catholicism by using the question-and-answer method of instruction.

In November 1884 the American bishops met for the Third Plenary Council of Baltimore, which was convened by Archbishop James Gibbons. During the final days of the two-month meeting, they commissioned Fr. DeConcilio to write a basic catechism that could be used for simple religious instruction. When this project was completed, the text of the catechism was forwarded to the bishops. They suggested numerous changes and so a revision was undertaken in 1896. The text was completely revised by 1941.

This catechism was the most popular religion text in Catholic schools and religious education programs until the 1960s. Many Catholic educators now consider it inadequate and outdated. Its theology has not been revised to reflect the developments in church thinking after Vatican II. Also the Baltimore Catechism's view of western culture and modern living is not in total harmony with the church's more recent teachings about the world and contemporary technology. (See also Catechesis, Confraternity of Christian Doctrine.)

BAPTISM   is the first sacrament received by all Catholic Christians. Through this sacrament, those baptized become members of the Body of Christ and the new people of god, the church. Baptism may be received only once and may be administered by infusion (a little water is poured on the head), or by immersion (the entire body is dipped in water). The words of baptism are: "I baptize you in the name of the Father, and of the Son, and of the Holy Spirit." The English term baptize is derived from a Greek verb that means "dipping in water." In the waters of baptism persons truly participate in the dying and rising to new life with Jesus the Lord. This is symbolized quite dramatically in the baptism of immersion.

Up to the middle of the 5th century most baptism candidates were adults. After long and prayerful preparations—"catechumenate" periods—candidates were immersed in water, and then confirmed by the local bishop in one ceremony. From the end of the 5th century until now, the church has stressed the need for infant baptism, has often delayed confirmation until preteen or teenage years, but has not usually stressed the need for intense preparation of baptism as it once did.

Current papal statements indicate that the church still regards infant baptism as the usual and more acceptable practice for Catholics to follow. The important role of parents and godparents, as representatives of the Catholic Church who will care for the child's needs and religious education, has been emphasized.

The Catholic Church calls all believers (and this has been especially stressed in recent decades), to view baptism as the first step in one's initiation into the Christian life. Guidelines for two separate ceremonies, one for adult converts and one for infants, have been published in recent years. Adults are expected to undergo a rather long stage-by-stage catechumenate period before receiving the sacrament of baptism. (For more information on this, study the document *The Rite of Christian Initiation of Adults*.) Baptisms now often take place during the celebration of the eucharist to highlight the close relationship between the sacraments of baptism and eucharist. A very special time for adult and infant baptisms is during the Easter Vigil ceremonies, on the Saturday night before Easter Sunday morning. (See also Baptistry, Catechumenate and the RCIA, Exorcism, Sacrament.)

BAPTISTRY is the separate room or place in the church where baptisms take place. The baptistry also refers to the basin or bowl-like container over which baptisms by water are performed.

From the 4th century until about 1000, baptistries were so large that the entire body of the person could be dipped (or immersed) in the water. When infant baptisms became popular, baptistrys were made smaller to allow for the pouring of just a little water over the foreheads of children. Many baptistrys contain images of Saint John the Baptist baptizing Jesus.

Since the baptism of infusion—pouring the small amount of water—is the most popular way to baptize infants and adults, most church baptistries are small fonts or basins, several feet tall, located in the front of a church or near the altar in the sanctuary. *Note of Interest:* The place for baptisms in modern churches is near the sanctuary and/or the altar. This is so because baptisms are now frequently celebrated during Mass. The church wishes to emphasize the close union between baptism and eucharist, two of the sacraments of initiation. Baptisms within Sunday Mass remind believers and worshippers that every Sunday is a time for rebirth and renewal. It is each church member's own "little Easter" celebration. Many baptistries are still located near the church's entrance, somewhere near the vestibule. These remind Christians of the early days of Christianity when "catechumens" were welcomed during the Easter Vigil ceremonies, into the People of God through the sacraments of baptism, confirmation, and eucharist. Baptisms were often performed in those early days in a pool of water placed just within the entrance to the church building. (See also Baptism, Sacristy, Vestibule.)

BEATITUDES   are a set of guides, or ways, which indicate the basic attitudes necessary to live an authentic Christian life. The Beatitudes can be found in Matthew, Chapter 5, and in Luke, Chapter 6. They introduce the Sermon on the Mount spoken by Jesus and tell how human beings should deal with troubles such as poverty, hunger, sorrow, and oppression in order to become blessed, worthy of the Kingdom of God.

The church teaches that Christians who live according to the Beatitudes are persons guided by the Holy Spirit. Those who live the beatitudes are always willing to serve the sick, the poor, and the unfortunate.

Here are the beatitudes listed in Matthew:

How blessed are the poor in spirit; the reign of God is theirs.

Blessed too are the sorrowing; they shall be consoled.

Blessed are the lowly; they shall inherit the land.

Blessed are they who hunger and thirst for holiness; they shall have their fill.

Blessed are they who show mercy; mercy shall be theirs.

Blessed are the single-hearted; they shall see God.

Blessed are the peacemakers; they shall be called sons of God.

Blessed are those persecuted for holiness' sake; the reign of God is theirs.

Blessed are you when they insult you and persecute you and utter every kind of slander against you because of me.

Be glad and rejoice, for your reward is great in heaven; they persecuted the prophets before you in the very same way. (See also Matthew, Morality, Works of Mercy.)

BENEDICTION OF THE BLESSED SACRAMENT is a short ceremony in which the consecrated host is shown to and adored by Catholics. A large host is usually placed in a gold container (a monstrance). The people gathered sing hymns and say special prayers, and the priest who leads the benediction ceremony blesses them with the monstrance.

This practice dates back to the 15th century and comes from a desire to display the blessed sacrament to Catholic Christians on important church feasts, such as the feast of Corpus Christi. Despite its long history, benediction was not accepted as an officially recognized liturgical action of the church until 1958.

Benediction is a ceremony that was developed to enrich the spiritual lives of church members. It is not, however, to be regarded as a substitute for the eucharistic liturgy or for receiving Jesus in the sacrament of the eucharist. Since the early 1960s the practice of celebrating benediction has declined. (See also Eucharist, Worship.)

BIBLE is a collection of 73 books that were written by numerous authors who were inspired by God. The word bible is derived from the Greek *biblia*, or "books." The bible is often referred to as the Word Of God or scripture. More copies of the bible have been printed, purchased, and read than any other book in history.

The first and longest part of the bible is called the Old Testament. The Old Testament reveals how people came to know the one true God. It was composed over many hundreds of years while the chosen people of Yahweh, the Hebrews, awaited the coming of a messiah. There are 46 books in the Old Testament.

The second major portion of the bible is called the New Testament. The New Testament is composed of 27 books that were written between A.D. 55 and the early 100s. The New Testament was written in Greek (whereas the Old Testament was written in Hebrew). The New Testament centers on the life, death, and resurrection of Jesus, and on the early community of his followers, whose mission was to preach and spread Jesus' good news of salvation to all humanity.

The bible is God's sacred inspired Word. God really guided the human writers to communicate important truths about himself. Many of the teachings of the Catholic Christian community are directly based upon the content of the bible. Catholics are encouraged to read the bible every day. (See also Bible, Books of; Inspiration; Revelation.)

BIBLE, BOOKS OF   There are 73 books in the bible, 46 in the Old Testament, and 27 in the New Testament. It was in the 16th century, during the Council of Trent, that church leaders made the critical decision about which books to include in the official "canon" of the bible. The following books are included, and only these. (The abbreviation of each book is in parentheses.)

Old Testament

The Law: Genesis (Gn) Exodus (Ex) Leviticus (Lv) Numbers (Nm) Deuteronomy (Dt).

The Prophets: Joshua (Jos) Judges (Jgs) 1 Samuel (1 Sm) 2 Samuel (2 Sm) 1 Kings (1 Kgs) 2 Kings (2 Kgs) Isaiah (Is) Jeremiah (Jer) Ezekiel (Ez) Hosea (Hos) Joel (Jl) Amos (Am) Obadiah (Ob) Jonah (Jon) Micah (Mi) Nahum (Na) Habakkuk (Hb) Zephaniah (Zep) Haggai (Hg) Zechariah (Zec) Malachi (Mal) Daniel (Dn).

The Writings: Ruth (Ru) 1 Chronicles (1 Chr) 2 Chronicles (2 Chr) Ezra (Ezr) Nehemiah (Neh) Esther (Est) Job (Jb) Psalms (Ps) Proverbs (Prv) Ecclesiastes (Ecc) Song Of Songs (Sg) Lamentations (Lam) Tobit (Tb) Judith (Jdt) Wisdom (Wis) Sirach (Sir) Baruch (Bar) 1 Maccabees (1 Mc) 2 Maccabees (2 Mc).

New Testament

The Gospels: Matthew (Mt) Mark (Mk) Luke (Lk) John (Jn) Acts of the Apostles (Acts)

The Epistles: Romans (Rom) 1 Corinthians (1 Cor) 2 Corinthians (2 Cor) Galatians (Gal) Ephesians (Eph) Philippians (Phil) Colossians (Col) 1 Thessalonians (1 Thes) 2 Thessalonians (2 Thes) 1 Timothy (1 Tim) 2 Timothy (2 Tim) Titus (Ti) Philemon (Phlm) Hebrews (Heb) James (Jas) 1 Peter (1 Pt) 2 Peter (2 Pt) 1 John (1 Jn) 2 John (2 Jn) 3 John (3 Jn) Jude (Jude).

Revelation (Rv). (See also Inspiration, New Testament, Old Testament.)

BIBLE WEEK   is a seven-day period set aside each year by the Laymen's National Bible Committee (LNBC) to urge members of all religions in the United States to read the bible, and to study and discuss the scriptures with others. The LNBC has members that are Catholic, Protestant, Jewish, Mormon, Christian Scientist, and Greek Orthodox.

National Bible Week has been held for 40 years. During this week the LNBC uses radio and TV spots and advertisements in magazines and local newspapers to recommend the reading and study of scripture. The National Bible Week celebration is held during the same week as Thanksgiving Day in November, a time when church-going citizens are asked to think about the meaning of freedom and the message of the bible.

The USCC (United States Catholic Conference) keeps an office called the Catholic Biblical Apostolate in Washington, D.C. This office, or center, yearly publishes a booklet about Bible Week to help promote the work of the LNBC and to help Catholics enjoy reading and learning about the bible.

BIRTH CONTROL/CONTRACEPTION   is any method used to prevent women from bearing children. Common types of birth control are artificial contraceptives, abortion, the rhythm method, and not having sexual intercourse at all. The teaching church sees the latter two methods as the only acceptable forms of birth control. However, the use of contraceptives such as "the pill," is permitted for a number of special medical reasons. Birth control is practiced by couples and individuals for economic, social, population-control, medical and religious reasons.

Early Church Fathers believed that *the* prime purpose of sex in marriage was procreation—having children. Throughout its history, the church has taught that using illicit means of birth control is a serious error. Many popes, such as Gregory IX, Pius XI, and Pius XII, have noted the evils of unapproved contraception.

The theology of marriage, which has developed over the years, accepts two prime reasons for sex in marriage: 1) the loving sharing of self with one's partner, and 2) procreation. Sexual acts have a special worth for humans that go beyond just having children. Also, it is now said that some uses of the ryhthm method and some of those who abstain from sex altogether for sound moral reasons show signs of mature, thoughtful parenting.

In 1964 Paul VI began a study of contraception that ended with the publication of *Humanae Vitae* in July 1968. He said that all sexual acts must be open to the possible creation of babies and added that Catholics may only use the rhythm method or the abstinence method for birth control. The church urged every Catholic to agree with this teaching. Many Catholics, though, did not agree with Pope Paul. The church reminds Catholics that they have a serious duty to reflect and pray before deciding to practice birth control against the teaching of the official church.

Note of Interest: Catholic Family Life programs advocate the use of the Billings birth control method. This method is easily learned, quite effective, and avoids using the pill (which has many harmful side effects). This is one modern method that is wholly approved by the church. (See also Free Will, Morality.)

BISHOP   is the usual leader of a local church community called a diocese. He serves as its spiritual leader and pastor. The word bishop is derived from the Greek *episkopos*, which means "one who is an overseer." The bishops of the church are the true successors to the apostles of Jesus. The College of Bishops—all the bishops in union with the pope—work together to teach, guide, serve, and care for the entire Catholic Church.

In the early church certain men were recognized as the leaders of their local communities either because they had been appointed by the apostles or because their communities had chosen them to act as overseers. Soon, however, local churches were led by one male overseer, a bishop. When issues and concerns arose that affected a number of churches in different parts of the Christian world, bishops held meetings called synods and councils to guide and direct church members. Local bishops were often elected by the people in their individual communities. In later years, however, it became the pope's task (and it still is his) to select and appoint bishops.

When he becomes a bishop, a man achieves the "fullness of the priesthood," the priesthood which began when he received the sacrament of orders. The bishop usually is the proper, ordinary, and immediate pastor of a local church called a diocese. He is sometimes referred to as the "ordinary" of the diocese; if he has other bishops who help him to lead and serve the diocese, these other men hold the title of "auxiliary" bishop. Catholic bishops are expected to care for their individual dioceses, but each of them also works as a kind of partner to other bishops to guide and care for the church on regional and national levels. Each is also part of the worldwide College of Bishops which—in union with the pope—leads and serves the church universal.

Bishops are the authentic successors of the apostles. They are teachers, leaders, guides, shepherds, but also the foremost servants of the church, the people of God. Some of their chief duties—in addition to watching out for the overall welfare of their dioceses—include preaching the gospel, instructing the faithful, presiding at liturgies, helping those who are needy, ordaining priests, and participating in the ordinations of other bishops.

Note of Interest: The bishops in the United States belong to the National Conference of Catholic Bishops (NCCB). This conference, or body of bishops, was established in 1966 and received the approval of the Vatican. The entire body of bishop-members of the NCCB gathers twice a year for formal meetings and discussions. The NCCB is the sponsor organization of the United States Catholic Conference, which is headquartered in Washington, D.C. (See also Apostles, Collegiality, Orders.)

CANDLES are used at Mass and in other church ceremonies as signs of the presence of the Spirit. They remind Catholics of the life of grace that they share, and lend a sense of dignity and holiness to the activities taking place. Candles are not used simply as substitute lights.

The earliest Christians often burned candles during funeral services and at the graves of martyrs. By the 7th century Christians were using lighted candles in processions at Masses. During the 11th century burning candles were placed on altars for Mass on a regular basis. In the 1600s the church decreed that some candles must be burning on the altar during every celebration of the Mass.

A blessing for candles has been part of Catholic life since the 15th century. It is becoming somewhat usual these days to bless only the paschal candle and the candles used at Mass. This blessing is given on February 2nd, Candlemas Day—officially, the feast of the Presentation. Generally the paschal candle and Mass candles must consist of more than 50% bleached beeswax. (See also Paschal Candle, Presentation, Vigil Lights.)

CANONIZATION is a process by which the church declares that a person who has died is in heaven and should be honored as a saint. In saying this, the church teaches that the person died a martyr for the faith or lived a Christian life worthy of imitation by all. Before a canonization takes place, the church conducts a complete study of the saint's life and history. He or she is first declared "blessed," then "beatified," and finally canonized.

Honoring martyrs at the sites of their graves during joyous ceremonies was a common practice of early Christians. Non-martyrs and very good Christians who were deceased, such as Martin of Tours, were being revered as saints by the late 300s. Since many people were thought to be worthy of sainthood by the 10th century, the church began the official process now known as canonization. The first canonized person was Saint Ulrich, who was named a saint by Pope John XV in 993. In 1588 Sixtus V asked a special commission to study the lives of holy men and women who had died and to advise him as to which of them should be canonized. This group still exists in the church and is called the Sacred Congregation for the Causes of Saints.

The complete listing of "blessed" persons and saints is in the current book of *Roman Martyrology*. In 1956 Butler published an unofficial lives of the Saints that listed over 2560 names. Between 1878 and 1977, the church declared over 175 persons saints, including Elizabeth Seton, Frances Cabrini, and John Neumann of the United States, and some Jesuits martyred in North America.

All persons who have entered the happiness of heaven are saints, not just those who have been canonized by the church. The process of canonization (as outlined in Canon Law), calls for full study of the candidate's life history and proof that miracles have taken place through the intercession of the person. After much prayer and thought, the pope names the candidate a saint of the Catholic Church and a feastday is selected for the new saint. (See also Heaven; Liturgical Year; Saints, Communion of.)

CANON LAW is a body of rules or norms drawn up for the correct administration and governing of all church matters. The term *canon* is based on an Egyptian word that refers to a measuring tool. The official volume of canon law is called *The Code of Canon Law,* which contains 2414 canons—or rules—to guide the church. The volume is divided into five books: 1) general laws, 2) laws for church members, 3) laws regarding sacred items, 4) laws about church trials, and 5) crime and punishment laws.

During the early Middle Ages, church rules were called the canonical order. By the 12th century, the rules were known as sacred canons. The first person to really study the full history of canon law was probably Ludovicus Thomassinus, a 17th century priest; thus, the Catholic Church's ability to do a complete, scientific study of canon law is a fairly new development. In 1904 Pius X believed that the church needed a new codification of all its rules. A group of cardinals, bishops, special consultants, and university professors worked on this huge project. By 1914 they had finished most of their work. The new *Code* was presented to Catholics by Benedict XV and went into effect on Pentecost Sunday in 1918.

Canon Law helps the church operate smoothly and is a guide that states the rights and duties of all church members. Rules are necessary but not always perfect, so canon law continues to develop.

In 1963 Pope John XXIII appointed a group of 29 cardinals (presently there are 41 in this group) to revise Canon Law. This updating of canons continues and though no date for publication has been set, it is widely expected that publication is to take place during 1982 or 1983. (See also Church, Laws of; Magisterium.)

CARDINAL is a member of that select group of bishops who are members of the Sacred College of Cardinals and who act as primary advisers and assistants to the pope. One of their main duties is to elect a new pope when necessary. The word cardinal comes from the Latin term *cardo*, which means "a hinge." Eugene IV said cardinals are like the hinges on which all church government turns. Cardinals are addressed as "Your Eminence," but in writing or speaking their full names, the word cardinal follows their first names, for example: Terence Cardinal Cooke, Archbishop of New York.

The first cardinals were bishops, priests, and deacons in 6th century Rome who helped elect the popes of that time. The college of Cardinals began in 1150, and during 1179, Alexander III decreed that only a pope could choose men to become cardinals of the church. The title of honor, "Eminence," was being used in the 17th century. Present-day cardinals are bishops of large archdioceses around the globe or are leaders of Roman Curia offices in the Vatican government. Since 1059 cardinals have been electing new popes in conclaves.

Canon Law (1918) states that all cardinals must be ordained priests. John XXIII ordered that they must also be bishops. Since 1586, there have been at least 70 cardinals of the church—perhaps a symbol of the 70 elders of the Hebrew people in the Old Testament. After a 1959 consistory (a meeting of the entire college with the pope), the church has had many more than 70 cardinals. Under Paul VI, for example, there were 145 cardinals by the year 1973.

The title "cardinal" is an honorary title, and there is a three-step process for creating a cardinal. First he is named by the pope at a secret consistory. Then he is told about his appointment in a *biglietto* (a notice). The third step is a special liturgy he celebrates with the entire college of cardinals in Rome. In 1971 it was decreed that cardinals who reach the age of 80 must retire and therefore can no longer participate in the elections of popes.

Note of Interest: 1) One deacon has been a cardinal of the church; his name was Giacomo Antonelli. 2) Sometimes a cardinal is chosen by the pope *in pectore* or *in petto*, which means the public is not informed of the choice. Some think that Pope John Paul II did this for a Chinese bishop late in 1979. (See also Bishop, Orders, Pope.)

CATECHESIS is a term derived from the Greek *katechein*, which means to "re-sound" or "re-echo." It also means "oral teaching." Catechesis is a form of the church's ministry of the word. Through catechetical activities Christian believers share their personal faith with other members of the community and/or with those who seek to join the church. True catechesis is much more than merely instruction about Catholic Christian beliefs. It is a sharing of personal faith by committed Christians so that the entire people of god (the church) may be continually converted to a fully Christian life, that is, turned away from sinfulness, centered on Jesus Christ, and living in hope for the perfected kingdom of God.

The term catechesis (in its Greek form) appears in the New Testament six times, and indicates a type of oral teaching about the Christian faith. In the very early church catechesis was used to prepare adults to enter the community of believers through baptism and the eucharist. These adults made up the church's "catechumenate." It is quite likely that catechesis continued once these catechumens had become full church members. This catechetical activity was called the *mystagogia* process; it was a time to ponder the great mysteries of the Christian faith. When the catechumenate disappeared, prior to the onset of the Middle Ages, the word catechesis was practically lost. At the time of the Protestant Reformation (16th century), a form of it returned in the word catechism. Catechisms were books used by church leaders to indoctrinate children, youth, and adult inquirers (converts) about the teachings, the rules, and the practices of the church. Often learners were expected to memorize and be able to orally repeat passages from these catechisms. For about four centuries (mid-1500s to mid-1900s), the Catholic catechism remained the primary tool for the religious instruction of Catholics. Two famous catechisms were the *Roman Catechism* (issued by Pope Pius V in 1566) and the *Baltimore Catechism*, produced in the United States during the late 1800s.

By the early 20th century a number of thinkers and teachers had begun to consider newer and better techniques for catechizing others. After Vatican II and the 1977 synod of bishops, the word catechesis once again became a familiar term for Catholics. In the 1960s Vatican II called for fresh approaches, methods, materials, etc., to help catechize. It commissioned the writing of a *General Catechetical Directory*, which appeared in 1971, to help catechists around the world. In 1979 the Catholic Church in the United States published a national catechetical directory *Sharing the Light of Faith*, which offers principles, guidelines, and ideas for catechesis.

Authentic catechesis shares the whole message of Christianity, the good news of the gospel, with others. Catechesis is centered on Jesus Christ and is aimed at all members of the church—adults, youth, children—to deepen and mature their faith. Catechesis is the responsibility of every church member: clergy, religious, and laity. It is ongoing: the life of every believer should be enriched by catechesis from his or her earliest to final years. In many places persons who serve as catechists receive formal training or updating in their teaching skills and theological knowledge in preparation for their ministry. Many parishes have persons who direct or coordinate the catechetical activities of their communities. These ministers are called directors of religious education (DREs) and coordinators (CREs).

Note of Interest: In July 1981 John Paul II noted that the "effectiveness of catechesis will depend largly on (our) capacity to give a Christian meaning to everything that makes up man's life in this time." The pope emphasized the significance of catechesis in families, parishes, schools, and through the mass media. He added the catechists' Christian witness must match their proficiency and skills in teaching doctrine. (See also Confraternity of Christian Doctrine, Faith, Witness.)

CATECHUMENATE AND THE RCIA is a period of time during which persons who wish to be full members of the Christian community proceed through four stages of initiation. The catechumenate is devoted to the spiritual, faith, and moral formation of men and women "catechumens." It guides them toward active and prayerful participation in church life and invites them to be faith-filled witnesses to Christ. During the 1960s Vatican Council II called for restoration and renewal of the catechumenate. In 1972 the *Rite Of Christian Initiation Of Adults* (RCIA) was published which describes the four stages and the liturgical celebrations (rites) that lead adults to full initiation into the church community. The term catechumenate derives from a Greek word, *katechein*, which means "to catechize, to teach orally."

The practice of initiating adult candidates into Christian life dates back to the earliest days of the church. Through the centuries, however, baptism of infants became the prevailing practice, and the important process of Christian initiation for adults and older youth was de-emphasized. Since then, with the publication of the *RCIA* in 1972, many dioceses and parishes throughout the country have begun again to initiate adults into church life through a real catechumenate.

The rites celebrated during the catechumenate period are designed to help the faith community discover the Spirit of God working in and through the adult candidates. It should thus experience authentic renewal of its own commitment to the Lord Jesus. Vatican II emphasized that catechumens must be led gradually to full incorporation into the church. The catechumenate guides them toward the prayerful reception of the sacraments of initiation, baptism, confirmation, and eucharist. Through this spiritual journey the church urges the entire faith community to deepen its trust in the gospel message and to be living witnesses to Christ. In some parish communities, the complete *Rite of Christian Initiation of Adults* is used during a nine-month period, which culminates with Lent, Easter, and the feast of Pentecost. The candidates receive the sacraments of initiation at the Easter Vigil liturgy. The four stages of the *RCIA* are:

1) *Precatechumenate* (Inquiry): The candidates seek to know what it takes to be a Catholic Christian. They are welcomed by the community and begin taking instruction.

2) *Catechumenate*: They learn how to follow Jesus and belong to the faith community. They accept church laws and norms.

3) *Illumination*: Candidates are *chosen* by the community to receive the sacraments of initiation and to become *enlightened*. The central celebration of the catechumenate takes place at the Easter Vigil ceremonies.

4) *Mystagogia*: They participate in post-baptismal catechesis. Through sharing the mysteries of faith, they attempt to help others grow in commitment to the Lord and the faith community.

The period of the catechumenate can be a prime time for catechesis and spiritual formation for all baptized Christians in the parish as well as for candidates. (See also Baptism, Confirmation.)

CELIBACY   is the voluntary state of being not married and abstaining from sexual intercourse. The celibate way of life is usually chosen by persons (clergy, religious, and laity) who wish to remain chaste and dedicate their lives, totally and unselfishly, to God, to the church, and to other people. Church law demands that priests be celibate. Members of religious orders are also expected to be celibates. The term celibacy comes from the Latin *caelibatus*, to live the single life.

Celibacy was freely chosen and practiced by some of the earliest Christians. By the 4th century a number of priests were required by church rules to remain celibate. In 1139 the 2nd Lateran Council taught that marriage is unlawful for all who receive the sacrament of orders. During the 16th century the Council of Trent formulated teachings on the discipline of celibacy and these teachings are currently followed by the Roman Catholic Church.

There has been discussion over the church's official celibacy laws in recent times. It has centered primarily on the real purpose of celibacy in the modern age. A number of church critics have argued that celibacy can and should be optional in some cases for priests. Vatican II stated that celibacy is a precious gift, held in high esteem by the church. It takes great commitment and sacrifice to faithfully live the celibate life. Some hold that the church should offer greater assistance to those who choose to be celibate.

Celibacy is a sign of total devotion to God and a sign of commitment to the good news of salvation. Saint Paul identified celibacy as a great aid to those Christians who want to focus their energies on serving others. Though celibacy is a requirement of church law for priests, it is possible that norms regarding it may change or be refined in the future. In 1979 John Paul II wrote a letter to priests to say that prayer will help them remain faithful to their commitment to the celibate life. (See also Orders, Religious Orders, Vows.)

CHARISMATICS are members of the Catholic Charismatic Renewal in the United States and all over the globe. They are sometimes called Catholic Pentecostals, members of a new Catholic pentecostal movement. The word charismatic has Greek roots and means *gifted*. The personal experience that charismatics share is called the "baptism of the Holy Spirit" through which God's Spirit recharges them and fills them with grace. It makes them enthusiastic Christians and gives them one or more special gifts, such as healing of the body or *glossolalia* (the ability to speak in tongues). Charismatics often meet weekly in small groups to pray, sing, share community spirit, and testify about personal faith moments.

The charismatic renewal gained momentum through the efforts of the Chi-Rho Society of Duquense University established in 1967. In the late 1970s over 3000 groups were meeting in the United States, and there were about 6,000,000 charismatics throughout the world. International meetings have been held for years at Notre Dame University. Charismatics publish the magazine *New Covenant*.

The charismatic movement encourages renewal of church life through the work of the Holy Spirit. It is an attempt to bring back the lively, spirit-filled attitude of post-Pentecost Christians. In 1976 American bishops gave cautious support to the movement, and Pope Paul VI also gave the Charismatics significant support.

The enthusiasm, fellowship, love for Jesus and scripture, sharing of personal gifts, and sharing with Protestant Christian groups can be very good for some people. It is important to remember that the church had not lost the Spirit before the charismatic renewal began. But the renewal is an excellent reminder of our need to rely on the Holy Spirit, and it has been a good influence on the church in general. (See also Pentecost, Trinity.)

CHARITY is one of the three theological virtues; the others are faith and hope. In his epistles Paul proclaims that charity is the greatest of all the virtues. This particular virtue enables people to love God and others unselfishly.

Over the years acts of charity have been performed by Christians in various ways. Sharing with the needy or with those who have problems are ways of being charitable. Offering prayers and good deeds for the souls in purgatory are signs of true charity. Showing love for those who are "enemies" is possible because of the virtue of charity. An important biblical quote on charity is Paul's passage, I Cor 13:4ff.

By loving God, all others, and ourselves too in unselfish ways, Catholics can make the kingdom of God on earth a living reality for all of humanity. Through charitable acts Christians can make the world a better place for the entire human race and are more able to give freely of themselves in order to love and help others.

True charity is a gift from God received by all Christians at the time of baptism. Willingness to love and serve God and to love, serve, and respect others is necessary in order to be saved. Pope John Paul II has stated that acts of Christian charity help the church to meet the real needs of the human race, especially the need to overcome poverty and to end physical hunger. (See also Social Justice, Virtue, Works of Mercy.)

CHRISTIAN UNITY WEEK is an annual 8-day period, January 18-25, during which Christians of various denominations—Catholics and non-Catholics alike—come together in prayer for the restoration of full unity among all Christian peoples.

This observance started with the "Chair of Unity Octave," which began officially in 1908 in the United States. Later, in 1935, a Frenchman named Abbé Paul Courturier retitled the octave "The Week Of Prayer For Christian Unity." He hoped that Christians united in prayer and spirit would "cause hearts to grow into one another, and finally unite minds in the eternal light of the one Christ." Courturier's work was authentic ecumenism. The observance of the octave retained a fairly heavy Roman Catholic, return-to-the-Roman-Church flavor, prior to Courturier's efforts, which turned off many non-Catholic Christians. In 1948 when the World Council of churches (WCC) was founded, it began to sponsor the Week of Prayer for Christian Unity. During the 1960s, with the publication of Vatican II's *Decree on Ecumenism*, all Catholics were encouraged to participate in this one, unified observance with other Christians. Some of the barriers and prejudices between Catholics and their "separated brethren" were lessened as a result. By 1966 a standard leaflet for the Week of Prayer was being published by the joint working group of the WCC and the Roman Catholic Church. In the United States, the Atonement Friars, at the Graymoor Ecumenical Institute in New York state, prepare Week of Christian Unity materials for Catholics.

Vatican II pointed out that separate Christian churches and ecclesial communions remain close to the Catholics of this world despite doctrinal and traditional differences. Church leaders and theologians at the council urged dialogue amoung church bodies and common prayer wherever and whenever possible. Also Vatican II asked each individual Christian to examine his or her trust in Christ's will for unity among all his followers, and then to undertake the vigorous work of renewal and reform among Christian peoples. (See also Ecumenism, Prayer.)

CHRISTMAS   is that day of the church year on which the birth of Jesus Christ is celebrated. The Christmas feast is set on December 25th and is a Catholic holy day of obligation. The word Christmas is based upon the old English *Cristes Maesse*, the "Mass of Christ."

The Christmas feast has been celebrated by Christians at least since the year 354. It was placed on December 25th to offset the pagan influences of a non-Christian winter solstice feast called "birthday of the sun."

Historians have discovered that Jesus Christ was probably born several years (maybe as many as seven) earlier than was originally thought. The mistake in identifying the actual birth year is probably due to Denis the Small, a 6th century monk, who began the practice of dating events in history "A.D."—*anno Domini*—which means "in the year of the Lord."

Christmastide begins for Catholics with a vigil, or evening Mass, on December 24th, and it continues until the Sunday following the feast of the Epiphany. The final day of Christmastide recalls and honors the baptism of the Lord and the beginning of his public ministry. The feast of Christmas is second in importance only to Easter for Catholic Christians. Priests are permitted to celebrate three Masses on the Christmas feast. The custom of having three Eucharistic celebrations for Christmas, one for the vigil, one for dawn, and one for the daytime, dates back to Saint Gregory the Great of the 6th century. (See also Christology, Liturgical Year.)

CHRISTOLOGY   is the study of Jesus Christ: who he is as a divine person, his divine and human natures, his mission and ministry to humankind, and his own consciousness of who he was in relation to God the Father. Catholics and other Christians hold that Jesus was the promised messiah, "the Christ," the second person of the Trinity who was incarnated in order to lead humanity to eternal salvation.

A number of church councils have studied Christology and have made formal declarations about Jesus Christ. The Council of Nicaea (Nicaea I, 325), attacked a heresy by Arius, which denied that Jesus was divine. The First Council of Constantinople (in 381), also attacked Arianism. In 431 the Council of Ephesus upheld belief in the essential unity of the divine and human natures in Jesus. In 451 the Council of Chalcedon, under the leadership of Pope St. Leo I, condemned the Monophysite heresy which claimed that Jesus had a divine nature but no human nature. Later, Nicaea II (in 787) proclaimed that Jesus really was the Son of God because of his divine nature rather than by "adoption."

Over the centuries Catholic thinkers and teachers have stressed belief in the Incarnation of the Second Person of the Blessed Trinity: 1) It has been held that he became human—was made flesh and that as a divine person he had united divine and human natures (called the hypostatic union). 2) It has been declared that Jesus Christ was conceived by the Holy Spirit (miraculously), and that he lived, died, and is risen from the dead, and as redeemer and mediator continues to offer unending salvation to all through his Spirit in the church.

Theologians refer to a Christology "from above" and a Christology "from below." The Christological thinking "from above" begins, basically, with the eternal, pre-existing Word of God (the *logos*) in heaven who proceeds to earth and offers salvation to fallen, sinful humankind (the theologies of John and Paul, for example, present a "from above" Christology). Christological thinking "from below" centers more on the historical Jesus who through his ministry on earth proves that he is sent to reconcile God and humanity and offer salvation to all (the Synoptic Gospels largely employ a Christology "from below").

The church stresses that the God-Man, Jesus Christ—a person who was prayerfully obedient, had faith in God, and love for all— was the messiah, the anointed Son of God. Often, Christology is distinguished from soteriology, which is the strict theological study of the saving works of the eternal redeemer. The teaching that Jesus was divine and human, and that he is the one, true Son of God, is central to all of Christian belief. Vatican II stressed (and the church continues to do so) that Jesus Christ is present through the Spirit in the church community. He is the sacrament of the encounter between the unseen God and humanity. Jesus Christ—a man among humans and God's own divine son—has perfected and completed divine revelation. As the new Adam, he is the head of the body of Christ, the mystery called the church. (See also Councils, Christological; Jesus, Titles of; Messiah; Trinity.)

CHURCH, IMAGES OF Many images or symbols are used to describe the reality we call church. Each image develops a particular aspect or element of the church, and taken together they show the richness, depth, and diversity of life within this community of Jesus Christ's followers. Vatican Council II used numerous images to describe the church (many of these can be found in the Council's *Dogmatic Constitution on the Church*, but some may also be located in other Vatican II documents). Listed below are some images of the church described by Vatican II.The church is a *mystery*. It is a reality that cannot be fully captured by human thought and words. In a 1963 address to Vatican II attendees, Paul VI noted that the church is a mystery imbued with the hidden presence of God. Like Jesus it is a historical, visible reality that manifests the true presence of the divinity. The more widely known images of the church follow.

People of God This image refers to the full community of church members with Christ at its head. This new and holy people is a lasting seed of unity, hope, and salvation for the whole human race, sent forth into the whole world as the light of the world and the salt of the earth. The people of God, the church, is a "new Israel," a sign of the new covenant between God and humankind. (See 1 Pt 2:9-10; Acts 20:28; Mt 5:13-16; 2 Cor 3:6.)

Community The Church is referred to as a true community of Christ's followers, especially in the celebration of the sacraments—communal worship—and through living the virtuous Christian life.

Mystical Body and *Body of Christ*. Just as each human being is a part of the entire body of humanity, so each church member is a part, in a mystical manner, of the whole of Christ's body (the church). As its head the risen Jesus is present in the community of believers and all the members of the church ought to be molded into Christ's image until he is formed in them. The Spirit of the Lord vivifies, unifies, and moves the whole body (See 1 Cor 12:12-13, 27-30; Col 3:15; Eph 4:4, 5:23.)

Sacrament In its relationship with the risen Jesus the church is a kind of sacrament of intimate union with God, and of the unity of all mankind. That is, the church is a sign and instrument of such union and unity. As a universal sacrament of salvation the church unites God and human beings, and also unites human beings with one another.

Temple of God. The "house of God" was founded on Christ and is the dwelling place of God among humans. In picturing the church as the holy temple, Vatican II compared individual Christians to living stones on earth that grow and develop as parts of the new kingdom of God. (See 1 Cor 3:9, 1 Tm 3:15, 2 Cor 6:16, Eph 2:19–22, Rv 21:3, 1 Pt 2:5.)

Sheepfold With Jesus as the good shepherd and prince of shepherds, the church is said to be a sheepfold, guided by human shepherds and ceaselessly led and nourished by the good shepherd himself. (See Jn 10:11–15; Is 40:11; Ez 34:11ff.; 1 Pt 5:4.)

Field of God and *Vineyard.* She is pictured as a tract of land to be cultivated and a choice vineyard. The true vine is the risen Jesus who gives life and fruitfulness to the branches who are members of the church body. (See Cor 3:9, Rom 11:13-26; Mt 21:33-43; Jn 15:1-5.)

Visible Structure The visible structure of the church interlocks in harmony with the spiritual community so that the church is comprised of a divine and human element, just like the one redeemer of humankind and head of the body, Jesus Christ. This image reminds believers that the church is an institution with a hierarchical structure.

Bride of Christ The church is depicted as Christ's one spouse. Having become the model of a man loving his wife as his own body, Christ loves the church as his bride. As such, the church is subject to its head so that it may grow and reach all the fullness of God. (See Eph 5:22–29, 3:19.) (See also Community, Ecclesiology, People of God.)

CHURCH, LAWS OF are seven important rules, among many norms, that all Catholics should know and are bound to keep. An original listing of six laws for American Catholics was issued at the Third Council of Baltimore in 1886. These laws were the same six observed in Great Britain and printed in 19th century English catechisms. Special rules such as fasting or making one's "Easter duty" date back to 9th century prayer books that were written in Europe.

In 1439 Saint Antoninus wrote about ten binding laws of the church. Later Saint Peter Canisius taught that there were five special church Laws. The official number of precepts was set at six by Saint Robert Bellarmine in 1589. The seventh rule, number three below, was recently introduced by American Catholic leaders. It urges all Catholics to take part in lifelong, continuing adult education—even after receiving Confirmation, the final sacrament of initiation.

The seven precepts or laws of the church for American Catholics are:

1. To keep holy the day of the Lord's resurrection; to worship God by participating in Mass every Sunday and holy day of obliga-

tion; to avoid those activities that would hinder renewal of soul and body, e.g., needless work and business activities, unnecessary shopping, etc.

2. To lead a sacramental life; to receive holy communion frequently—minimally, to receive holy communion at least once a year, between the first Sunday of Lent and Trinity Sunday; to receive the sacrament of penance regularly—minimally, to receive the sacrament of penance at least once a year (annual confession is obligatory only if serious sin is involved).

3. To study Catholic teaching in preparation for the sacrament of confirmation, to be confirmed, and then to continue to study and advance the cause of Christ.

4. To observe the marriage laws of the church; to give religious training (by example and word) to one's children; to use parish schools and religious education programs.

5. To strengthen and support the church; to support one's own parish community and parish priests; to support the worldwide church and the Holy Father the Pope.

6. To do penance, including abstaining from meat and fasting from food on the appointed days.

7. To join in the missionary spirit and apostolate of the church. (See also Canon Law.)

COLLEGIALITY   is a term that refers to the power held by the bishops of the church, in union with the pope, to teach and guide all Catholics. Just as Saint Peter and the other apostles worked together as a *college,* or community, so their true successors—the pope and bishops—work together in order to lead the church.

By the 5th century collegiality was a term commonly used by Catholic leaders to denote the unity of the bishops who governed church matters. Though the pope is the authentic head and primary leader for all Catholics, it is the pope and the bishops together who guide Catholic Christianity as true shepherds and concerned pastors.

The term "collegiality" was given a special, renewed honor at the Second Vatican Council. The pope remains the central authority for all Catholics but the bishops and the pope must continue to work in harmony—as a hierarchy—in order to inform and direct the life of the church on earth. This united effort to lead the church is good and much more thought and study will be done about how to best put collegiality into practice on a regular basis.

Teachings on collegiality were actually formalized by Vatican Council II. The pope—chief leader of all Catholic Christians and the Bishop of Rome—plus the other bishops were charged with the responsibility of caring for their individual dioceses and for the entire church community on earth. This college of church authorities is expected to teach authentic doctrines, govern Catholics regarding issues of faith and morals, and to help sanctify Catholics, especially by seeing that they enjoy ample opportunities to receive the seven sacraments. (See also Bishop, Pope, Synod of Bishops.)

COMMANDMENTS OF GOD   are ten rules that are found in the Old Testament in Dt 5:6–21 and Ex 20:1–17. The Ten Commandments are sometimes called the Decalogue. It is taught in scripture that God the Father (Yahweh) gave these guides for the moral and religious life of his chosen people to their leader Moses.

The Ten Commandments are important guides followed by all faithful Christians and Jews to this day. The first three center on humanity's relationship to God: 1) human beings must not believe in false gods 2) should honor the holy name of God, and 3) must keep holy the Sabbath—observed by Christians on Sunday—as a day of worship and rest from daily labors. The remaining seven commands center on person-to-person relationships. Men and women are called to respect parents and other authorities, to respect all individuals' right to life, to refrain from illicit sexual activities, to avoid thievery (stealing). In addition they are cautioned never to deny anyone justice, to tell the truth, and to respect the marriages and possessions of others.

The Catholic Church teaches that God made a covenant with the Hebrew people during Old Testament days but he has established a new covenant with the new people of God, the church, through Jesus Christ the savior. This new, loving agreement between God and humankind will last until the end of time. Jesus demanded that his followers adhere to two fundamental commands, upon which all other commandments rest: To love God totally with heart, mind, and soul, and to love all others as they love themselves.

The Ten commandments are: 1) I, the Lord, am your God; you shall have no other gods besides me. 2) You shall not take the name of the Lord your God in vain. 3) Remember to keep holy the sabbath day. 4) Honor your father and your mother. 5) You shall not kill. 6) You shall not commit adultery. 7) You shall not steal. 8) You shall not bear false witness against your neighbor. 9) You shall not covet your neighbor's wife. 10) You shall not covet anything that belongs to your neighbor. (See also Morality, Moses, Old Testament.)

COMMUNITY   is a unified group of individuals who share common beliefs, values, and tasks or responsibilities. Catholics are members of the community called the Catholic Christian Church and, together, follow the teachings and commands of God and his Son, Jesus Christ.

During Old Testament times, the Hebrews were the community, or "people of God" who shared a loving covenant agreement with Yahweh. The new community, or new people of God, was established by Jesus and has spread to all parts of the world. It is Jesus' basic teachings, his values, and his command to help all persons hear the good news of salvation that guide Catholic Christians in their day-to-day activities.

The meaning of community was very important to church fathers who attended Vatican Council II. Members of the church were urged then—and are urged now—to think of themselves as community persons who are part of a unified body of Christ—members of the Mystical Body of Christ. In recent years the church has been referred to as a true community of faith. The Holy Trinity as a unity or community of three divine persons Father, Son, and Holy Spirit is a model for church community.

Vatican II stated very clearly that all persons are meant to live, and have a strong desire to live, with others. This council taught that the church—the new people of God—should always remain a united and "single people," a community that loves God and serves him every day in thought, word, and action.

Note of Interest: Basic Christian Communities are being formed throughout the United States. Inspired by the Hispanic *comunidades eclesiales de base* models, these communities are relatively small neighborhood churches or grass-roots groups that serve as alternatives to larger, impersonal, highly traditional parish structures. Basic Christian communities are composed of individuals and families who value close personal relationships with other active Christians, the experience of authentic community, the opportunity to serve and minister to others, and the sharing of faith that is nourished by reflection on the gospels, social action, and prayerful celebration of the sacraments.

Several factors have led to the development of basic Christian communities in this country: real dissatisfaction with the usual, often impersonal parish model of local church; the shortage of ordained ministers in some geographical areas; and the relative isolation of some rural Catholics. The *comunidades eclesiales de base* are quite important to Catholic and Protestant churches around the globe, especially in Latin America, Africa, and Asia. In his apostolic exhortation, *Evangelii Nuntiandi*, Paul VI showed interest and support for such basic communities, noting that they can indeed become authentic proclaimers of the gospel message. (See also Church, Images of; People of God.)

CONFESSIONAL is a small booth or compartment where Catholics confess their sins to a priest and receive absolution privately and anonymously. Usually the person who is confessing a sin in the confessional kneels, separated from the priest by a thin curtain or screen.

During the early days of the church Christians often admitted their sinfulness and need for forgiveness to other members of the church. Private confessions to a priest and private penances became very popular in later years and the use of confessionals became widespread after the Council of Trent in the 16th century. Saint Charles Borromeo, a cardinal in Milan Italy (during the 16th century), was probably the first church leader to place a confessional in a church.

Confessionals are used by Catholics even to this day to insure that sins will be heard privately and anonymously. Priests are bound by church law to keep all sins confessed—whether within or outside a confessional—completely secret for all time. This is referred to as the seal of confession. Should a priest tell someone about a specific person's sin, heard during a Catholic's confession, the church excommunicates him (removes him from the church community).

Note of Interest: A reconciliation room, which is sometimes referred to as a confession room, is an area set aside in the church for the celebration of reconciliation (the sacrament of penance). The reconciliation room should provide a warm, welcoming environment—carpets and drapes, comfortable furniture, decorative artwork, pleasant colors and lighting. The one who enters the room to confess his or her sinfulness and to receive sacramental absolution may choose to sit opposite the priest for face-to-face confession or may elect to sit or kneel with grillwork or a curtain separating him or her from the priest. This inviting environment emphasizes God's great mercy, comforting love, and forgiveness. (See also Actual Sin, Reconciliation, Sin.)

CONFIRMATION is a sacrament of initiation, one of the church's seven sacraments. Confirmation may be received only once. This sacrament strengthens baptized Christians and through the gift of the Holy Spirit helps them to be active, caring followers of Jesus. It helps them become willing to witness to personal faith, to proclaim the good news of Christ, and to serve others. A Catholic bishop, the normal and original minister of confirmation, confers this sacrament by praying to the Holy Spirit, placing his hands over each person to be confirmed, and saying, "Be sealed with the gift of the Holy Spirit." He also anoints the one confirmed with holy oil (chrism) by tracing the sign of the cross on his or her forehead.

In the early church, when most converts were adults, Christians were usually baptized and confirmed during the same ceremony. As Christianity grew and gained new members, adult converts as well as infants and children were baptized by priests and later confirmed by bishops. Since the Middle Ages the Roman Catholic Church has offered the sacrament of confirmation to young Catholics just entering their teenage years and to adult converts to the faith. In the Eastern Catholic Church persons are still baptized and confirmed in the same ceremony.

Confirmation is a step in each Christian's initiation into the church community. It is called a personal Pentecost and the sacrament of maturity. Christians receive God's Spirit and grace through confirmation. The chrism used to anoint believers is a sign of the strengthening each needs to be an active, faith-filled followers of Jesus.

Two significant issues about confirmation have not been resolved by modern Catholics. 1) Is there a better or more proper age for receiving confirmation? 2) Should the original order of conferring the sacraments of initiation: baptism first, then confirmation, and then the eucharist, be restored by the church? These issues are being studied and discussed by concerned clergy, religious, and lay members of the church. Also study, research, and practical use of the recent document *The Rite of Christian Initiation of Adults* will help answer these questions. Many Catholic theologians, educators, and other ministers see great potential in this new ritual for the preparation and initiation of new church members. (See also Anointing, Catechumenate and the RCIA, Sacraments.)

CONFRATERNITY OF CHRISTIAN DOCTRINE (CCD)   is dedicated to the religious education of all children and older youth not reached by Catholic schools, youth, and adult members of the Catholic Church.

The first CCD programs were begun by Pope Pius IV in the city of Rome during the year 1560. Eleven years later Pius V decreed that this type of instruction was good for the entire church, and so he urged other bishops to initiate CCD programs in their dioceses. In 1905 Pius X stated that the CCD is intended to instruct all church members who do not know basic Christian teachings. The next pope, Pius XI, added that all Catholic parish communities should have CCD programs. This teaching became part of official Canon Law in 1935.

The CCD headquarters in the United States was founded at the United States Catholic Conference (USCC) in 1933, in Washington D.C. From 1969 to early 1982, the CCD office in the USCC Department of Education was guided by the individual who was also the executive secretary to the National Conference of Diocesan Directors of Religious Education (NCDD). The NCDD left the conference in Washington in 1982 to become an independent organization. There remains an official representative for Catechesis at the USCC, but the representative no longer functions as NCDD Executive Secretary.

The three primary goals of CCD programs in parishes are: 1) religious education programs for adults; 2) religious education for children, older youth, and their parents; 3) religion programs for all persons who remain outside the life of the church.

In recent years much emphasis has been placed on the critical need for adult education, adult catechesis, and renewed efforts at evangelization in Catholic parish communities. Lay persons and religious men and women, as from the very beginning of the CCD movement, continue to comprise the majority of all religion teachers/catechists in parish religious education programs.

Note of Interest: Three important official documents for all persons involved in religious education/CCD programs are: *Sharing the Light of Faith: National Catechetical Directory for Catholics in the United States; To Teach as Jesus Did; Basic Teachings for Catholic Religious Education.* All of these were prepared by the National Conference of Catholic Bishops, and are published by the United States Catholic Conference in Washington D.C. (See also Catechesis, Parish, United States Catholic Conference.)

CONVERSION is a process by which a person becomes more and more devoted to the good news of Christ and salvation, and centers his/her life on charity, service to others, and prayerful communication with God. Conversion is sometimes called *metanoia*, which means a basic change of mind and heart. The word conversion is rooted in the Latin *conversio*, which suggests a turning or a turning around of one's life.

In the gospels and in Acts of the Apostles, the fundamental call of Jesus and his apostles to others is to repentance, conversion, and faith—for the kingdom of God is at hand (Mk 1:15, Acts

2:38). In the early church persons who wished to convert to the Christian way of life were prepared for full membership through a catechumenate period, reception of the sacraments, and post-baptismal catechesis. A Christian was someone who experienced ongoing conversion and maturing faith, one who believed in Christ wholly, and whose complete life was transformed by such faith. In later centuries a convert mentality crept into the church: adults and youth who wished to become Catholics were known as converts. Preparation for their conversion centered on the study of church doctrines and practices rather than in-depth preparation for dynamic, lifelong conversion.

Since life is more like a journey, baptized people of God should become more and more converted, turned away from sinfulness, and turned toward the message of Christ and mission of his body, the church. Vatican Council II taught that the Christian who experiences conversion, through the interior work of the Spirit, witnesses to a changed outlook on life and is more open to God's love, and willing to serve others in a spirit of charity.The church teaches that prayer and the sacraments should be central in the lives of maturing Christians, especially the eucharist and the sacrament of penance.

Note of Interest: Through the *Rite of Christian Initiation of Adults*, issued in 1972, many adults are now actively prepared for membership in the church and for the lifelong process of conversion and commitment to Jesus Christ and his community. (See also Catechumenate and the RCIA, Grace, Reconciliation.)

COUNCILS, CHRISTOLOGICAL　　are six ecumenical councils that dealt with important and lasting doctrines about Jesus Christ. The names of these six councils, including some pertinent facts about each, and a synopsis of each's position on heresies about Jesus Christ, follow:

Nicaea I was held in 325 while Sylvester I was pope. About 300 bishops of the church attended. Nicaea I was actually called by the Roman Emperor Constantine in order to deal with the heresy (false teaching) of Arius, called Arianism. This heresy denied the true divinity of Jesus. Nicaea I did condemn the teachings of Arius and declared him a heretic. The council proclaimed that Jesus was actually divine and human.

Constantinople I took place in 381, with about 150 bishops participating, during the time of Pope Damasus I (though he personally did not attend the council). The famous Nicene Creed, which Catholics pray at the Sunday liturgy, is credited to Constantinople I. New forms of Arianism and another heretical teaching, which denied the divine nature of the Holy Spirit, were condemned by this council.

Ephesus, held in 431, was organized by the Emperor Theodosius II. About 200 bishops participated in the five general sessions of this council, and Saint Celestine I was pope at the time. He was represented at the Council of Ephesus by some delegates. This council condemned the heresy of Nestorius who denied the union of Christ's divine nature and human nature in one person.

Chalcedon was held in 451. About 600 bishops attended its 17 general sessions. Saint Leo I (Leo the Great) was the pope. This council condemned monophysitism, also known as Eutychianism (after the false teaching of Eutyches), which claimed that Jesus Christ had a divine nature but did not really have a human nature. In effect it denied the humanity of the Lord Jesus.

Constantinople III took place in 680, with about 170 bishops attending the 16 general sessions. Constantinople III condemned a heresy which maintained that Jesus Christ had a divine will but no human will. Agathonus and Leo II were the popes involved with this particular council.

Nicaea II occurred in 787, when Adrian I was pope; about 300 bishops participated in this council's eight sessions. Nicaea II cited and condemned the errors of adoptionism, a false doctrine which held that Jesus was the Son of God by adoption but not through his divine nature. (See also Christology; Council, Ecumenical; Magisterium.)

COUNCILS, ECUMENICAL are meetings of Catholic bishops from around the world who come together in order to teach, direct, guide, and sanctify the universal church. Whenever these bishops meet in such a council they act—in unity with the pope—as a collegial body that has full and supreme power to lead all church members. The pope (the Bishop of Rome and the chief shepherd of the church) convenes an ecumenical council, decides the topics that should be studied, functions as the head of each session, and accepts or confirms the declarations of the council meeting.

The first church council was the meeting of the apostles in Jerusalem in the year 52. Other very important ecumenical church meetings have included: 1) the Council of Nicaea, 325; 2) the Fourth Lateran Coucil, 1215; 3) the Council of Trent, 1542–1563; 4) Vatican Council I, which concluded in 1870; and 5) Vatican Council II, 1962–1965, which was the most recent ecumenical council. Over the centuries there have been 21 councils which are recognized as ecumenical councils of the Catholic Church.

A council is truly "ecumenical" when the community of church leaders in attendance considers matters that concern the universal church. They issue formal declarations and decrees that are binding for all Catholic persons. This college of bishops, in union with the pope, is called to use full and supreme authority to lead the church during an ecumenical council. The pope alone (outside the council) is also able to exercise full and supreme power in the church as its head and primary pastor. Church thinkers continue to freely discuss and debate the many ways in which the pope and other bishops exercise supreme power to lead and guide Catholics around the globe.

The church holds that the official teachings and decrees of ecumenical councils express the beliefs of the whole Catholic community. With the guidance of the Holy Spirit, the pope decides when it is necessary to have a general council. The bishops who attend the council (again with the guidance of the Holy Spirit), unite as a body to study and resolve the matters facing Catholics, in order to effectively teach and guide the whole church. Cardinals, archbishops, bishops, patriarchs, and other church leaders may cast votes during the council meetings. Other persons, including theologians and laypersons, may attend and sometimes even speak at ecumenical councils, but these persons cannot vote on matters at hand. The most recent ecumenical council was Vatican Council II, which was convened by John XXIII. Approximately 2800 church leaders attended this council; sixteen major documents that outline important church teachings were produced by Vatican II.

Note of Interest: Sometimes a group of church leaders meets for regional, national, and provincial church councils. These are referred to as *particular* councils (rather than ecumenical councils), since they are called in order to deal with issues concerning only one part or one segment of church life. The decisions reached during particular council meetings are not usually binding upon the universal Catholic Church. (See also Bishop, Vatican Council II.)

COVENANT   is the holy love relationship or agreement between God and his people. Through this agreement humankind receives God's gift of grace, and men and women are enabled to offer their complete lives to him and to charitable service for others in his name.

In ancient times covenants were agreements (something like business contracts), between two or more parties, which were finalized at special ceremonies or sacred actions. The Hebrews of the Old Testament agreed to a covenant friendship that was much more than a mere business contract. It was an agreement based on true love and respect offered by their God, Yahweh. The Hebrews believed that holy friendship such as this was to last forever. There was a series of loving, sacred covenants established between Yahweh and the Hebrew people. Some of the great figures associated with these covenant agreements are Abraham, Noah, and Moses. Misfortune and great sorrow befell the people whenever the basic loving agreement with Yahweh was broken.

The church holds that Jesus Christ, the Son of God, is the person who fulfilled the original covenant relationship between God and the human race. By his death and resurrection Jesus began a new covenant. This new relationship promises life and friendship with God forever if Christians accept Jesus' teachings, follow him, and lead moral lives. The most sacred action that Catholics use to express and celebrate this new covenant with God is the eucharist, or the Mass.

Catholics believe that only God can initiate a sacred covenant relationship. Humanity must respond to the Father's offer of friendship and lasting happiness in order for the covenant to continue. (See also Hebrews, People of God, Yahweh.)

CREATION   is the act of bringing something from nothing. The church's doctrine on creation teaches that God is good, that he is the source of all that has being, and that he has created the universe from nothingness. The church teaches that through creation God freely chose to show his great glory and love to all his creatures.

The biblical account of creation is found at the beginning of the Old Testament in Genesis 1:1–2:4. This account indicates that God created the entire universe from nothing in six separate acts, or on "six days" of creative activity. Humanity was placed at the highest level of created order and human beings were made in God's own image and likeness. During the history of the church, Catholics have received significant teachings about creation— from the Fourth Lateran Council (1215), the Council of Florence (1438–45), from Vatican I (1870), and from Vatican II in the *Constitution on the Church in the Modern World*. A most beautiful portrayal of God's creation was done by the artist Michaelangelo, in the early 1500s, in the Sistine Chapel of the Vatican.

Creation is the first step in God's divine plan of salvation and it is an on-going, enduring relationship between God and his creatures, especially humankind. The modern church honors the true dignity of human work and other creative activities, since through labor humanity participates in and cooperates with God's creation. The church recognizes that there need no be conflict between scientific studies of the world's origins and the Catholic doctrine of creation.

The church maintains that creation is a sign of God's loving self-giving. God is all good and so he has freely chosen to create everything that is. All of reality, including that which is spiritual and that which is material, is good because God has created it so (see Gn 1:31). A number of heresies, which the church has condemned forcefully throughout history, have centered on the notion that created matter is essentially evil. (See also Adam and Eve, Old Testament, Original Sin.)

DAVID, KING   is called the greatest of Israel's kings. His Hebrew name means prince or beloved one. He was the youngest of Jesse's eight sons. Because of his bravery and strong leadership, he is remembered by many Christians and Jews as the most ideal ruler of the Hebrew people. David lived about 1000 years before the birth of Jesus.

When he was quite young David was asked to play his harp for King Saul who was very depressed. Saul cheered by David's music, thanked him by making him a soldier in his army. During an important battle, David killed a Philistine giant named Goliath, and so became very popular with the Israelites. Saul was jealous of David's success, and he tried to have him killed. Fearing for his life, David hid in the desert. When Saul died—approximately 1000 B.C.—David was named king of one-half of Israel. A seven-year war with the other Israelite king—Saul's son Ishball and his general, Abner—was won by David. He became the sole king of Israel with his home base in Jerusalem.

David was a great religious and political leader who was the special choice of Yahweh to lead the Hebrew nation. Many Christians remember David as a great king but also as an example of a penitent and contrite person. While he was king, David committed sins of adultery and murder. He confessed his sins, did penances, and trusted that God had forgiven him.

Jesus was descended from the "house of David" since Saint Joseph, the husband of Mary, was a member of David's family. The prophet Nathan predicted that David's kingship would last forever despite sin and evil deeds. The greatest king of the new people of God is Jesus who restored the dynasty of the house of David. By his death and resurrection, he created God's new nation or people, the church. (See also Saul, Solomon, Zionism.)

DEACONS are persons who are ordained by bishops to a rank in the Catholic hierarchy just below the priests. The word deacon comes from the Greek *diakonia*, which means "helper" or "server."

The first deacons were chosen by the apostles to help with day-to-day matters in their communities. Clement of Rome, a first century bishop and saint, noted that deacons were the very first fruits or harvest of the 12 apostles. Deacons helped seat people in churches prior to Mass, read the bible during liturgies, preached on the scriptures, and distributed the eucharist.

In recent years the diaconate has again become a special and important church ministry. A large number of Catholic men— some celibate, some married with families, have been ordained deacons in the United States. Married men are called permanent deacons. Seminarians who are stydying for the priesthood are called transitional deacons.

To be ordained a transitional deacon a man must be at least 25 years old and must promise that he will never marry. To be ordained a permanent deacon he must be at least 35 years of age, and if married, must promise never to remarry should his wife die. The church teaches that these Catholic men have a special calling to build up and serve the church and the world. Deacons are often asked to assist the priest at the altar during Mass and to distribute communion. By an agreement with the local bishop, some deacons receive the right to preach during liturgies, give witness to marriage ceremonies, and to perform baptisms. (See also Ministry, Orders.)

DEAD SEA SCROLLS is the popular name given to writings found in the caves of the Qumran desert (near the Dead Sea), in 1947. These writings are important to Catholics because they shed light on little known Jewish history from 100 B.C. to A.D. 60. The scrolls have been described as one of the greatest finds for the church in this century.

The scrolls found at Qumran include the actual texts of the books of the Old Testament, excluding the book of Esther. Special finds have included the complete book of Isaiah and some "Messiah" writings about one who was to come to save Israel at a time called the apocalypse.

Since 1947 hundreds more scrolls have been excavated from the Qumran caves. These scrolls describe the way people lived during Jesus' lifetime. Since the original copies of many books of the bible can no longer be found, the Dead Sea Scrolls are the best available copies of these writings. (See also Bible, Books of.)

DEATH/DYING   is the climactic experience of human existence through which human beings fully encounter the one true God. The church teaches that death does not equal extinction because the human self lives on after physical death. Humans are created to enjoy the happiness of life beyond this earth, and all of human existence should be aimed at and summed up in the possibility of meeting God beyond natural time. It requires great faith to trust that only through death can full and free life with God be enjoyed. However, many persons feel anxiety and fear about death due perhaps to sinfulness and imperfect faith in God.

It is clear from the book of Genesis in the Old Testament as well as church tradition, that all the suffering associated with human death was not part of God's plan for humankind. Death is related to sin and its sufferings can be traced to original sin. Yet the people of God recognize that Jesus the risen Lord has conquered sin and death once-and-for-all (See Heb 2:14–18). Jesus offers the good news of eternal salvation to every person, and he will return in glory at the end of time. During the first Christian centuries Athanasius and John Chrysostom among others stressed that through his resurrection Jesus won a great victory over the power of sin and death. At the Council of Trent (in the 16th century), church leaders taught that the sin of Adam, original sin, introduced death into human experience as a penalty for sin (See Rom 5:12–14). The church's traditional belief in a particular judgment (each person is judged by God at the point of death) has served to underscore that human death is really final and that living a faith-filled, moral life is crucial for eternal happiness.

Some modern theologians believe that at the moment of death each person makes a decision for or against God, thus irreversibly shaping one's ultimate destiny. Other theologians believe that since death is an inescapable part of human reality, the moral choices of a lifetime, are the key factors that determine one's ultimate end.

Vatican Council II taught that faith alone helps human beings to allay some of the fears associated with death and center on the hope of an eternal life (See 2 Cor 5:1). In the *Constitution on the Church in the Modern World*, the council taught that human beings abhor the absolute ruin and total disappearance of their earthly existence, yet through Christ's victory over death, they are called to be joined to him in an endless sharing of a divine life beyond all corruption. In 1979 the Vatican issued a *Letter on Certain Questions Concerning Eschatology* which upheld long-standing church teachings on the individual's existence after death, the resurrection of the dead at the end of natural time (See Rom 8:11), and the purpose of prayer for those already dead. The church community offers baptism, reconciliation, eucharist, and anointing of the sick to persons who are dying, which reminds them that through Christ and in Christ, the riddles of sorrow and death grow meaningful. Apart from his gospel, these riddles overwhelm them. Christ has risen, thereby destroying death, and they can indeed place their complete trust and hope in God. (See also Anointing of the Sick, Faith, Original Sin.)

DIVORCE is a judgment rendered by a civil court that the marriage of a man and woman no longer exists. Catholics hold that a true and valid marriage can never be ended while both partners are alive. Sometimes Catholics do seek legal divorces but they must also obtain an official annulment of their first marriage before they may be remarried.

In the New Testament Jesus teaches that any man or woman who is divorced and then remarries commits adultery (for example, see Mk 10:6-12 and Lk 16:18). It seems likely that Jesus based his moral teachings on divorce, at least in part, on the book of Genesis. Paul outlines early Christian teaching on divorce more fully in his first letter to the Corinthians (see 1 Cor 7:10-11). Over the centuries the church has continued to teach that a valid marriage does not end until either the husband or wife dies. The Council of Trent, in the 16th century, restated that any person who remarries after previously entering into a valid marriage is guilty of the sin of adultery.

A valid marriage is a covenant agreement between a man and a woman. The covenant continues to exist even though a couple may be separated or legally divorced. The church urges divorced persons—and those thinking about divorce and/or remarriage—to talk with a priest, or some other knowledgeable Catholic about the conditions for a valid marriage and the process for obtaining official church annulments. While holding that no valid marriage can be ended easily, the church does not rule out separation and legal divorce when these will protect the rights, safety, and dignity of Catholics in troubled marital relationships. The church offers in-depth programs to engaged couples to help them better prepare for the wedding ceremony and for married life in general.

A person who is simply divorced and remarried cannot receive the sacraments but may attend all church worship services. Catholics who are divorced must always receive an annulment prior to validly marrying another partner. The church encourages divorced and remarried Catholics to seek special guidance and help from the church as they live their lives.

Note of Interest: There is a growing active ministry to separated, divorced, and remarried Catholics in the church today. This ministry offers parish support, study groups, counselling services, diocesan family life services, and even national support through workshops and meetings of Catholics who are separated, divorced, and/or remarried. (See also Annulment, Family Ministry, Matrimony.)

DOCTRINE is official church teaching. The word is often used to designate the entire body of church teachings as in "Catholic doctrine." The term comes from the Latin *docere*, which means teaching or instructing. Doctrines are derived from scripture, from the faith life of church communities, from traditional beliefs and moral practices. They are defined and proclaimed, authentically and authoritatively, by the magisterium of the church.

Doctrines center on truths revealed to and cherished by the followers of Jesus Christ. Church teachings can be classified as either doctrines or as dogmas of Catholicism. Doctrines center on great truths and mysteries accepted and believed by church members. Dogmas express truths revealed directly by God and, as infallible teachings, are more authoritative than individual doctrinal statements. In the entire body of church teachings, all dogmas are doctrines of faith declared by the church, but not all doctrines carry the authority of dogmas. Doctrines do undergo development through the years. Though important truths that are expressed in any single doctrine can never be altered, the words and ways in which the doctrine is proclaimed may be changed and perfected in order that men and women can better understand and accept the teaching.

Vatican Council II noted that doctrines are part of a living church tradition that helps the faithful grow in the understanding of the realities and the words which have been handed down to believers since the time of the apostles. In the process of defining official doctrines, the church constantly moves forward toward the fullness of divine truth. Doctrines remain alive and significant for Catholics only as long as they are explained, taught, dialogued about, and reformed by and for church members. Doctrines should be "rethought" at all times, so that they can be more aptly and clearly stated, and so that they will continue to help the faithful uncover the deep truths to which doctrinal formulas point.

Official doctrines are a basis of the Christian way of life and not just dry teachings to which a person should assent in intellect alone. Doctrines are proclaimed by the magisterium in order to present and conserve divine truths. [In using magisterium here, it is assumed that doctrines can be officially defined by 1) the pope alone, 2) the whole, united college of bishops in union with the pope, and 3) bishops seeking to instruct the faithful.] The church maintains that there is a hierarchy of truths with dogmas taking the highest places on such a listing. In 1978 Pope John Paul I recognized that doctrinal formulas sometimes need updating. Earlier Paul VI wrote that the church must continue to correct doctrinal errors, and set straight teachers of false doctrines. He urged all Catholics to condemn incorrect teachings. Since 1965 a commission known as the Congregation for the Doctrines of the Faith has functioned at the Vatican. The task of this commission is to promote and safeguard authentic teachings on faith and morality. (See also Catechesis, Dogma, Tradition.)

DOGMA   is a solemnly defined, infallible teaching of the Catholic Church. The church holds that dogmatic truths have been revealed by God and therefore must be fully accepted by all members. Derived from the Greek, the word dogma means "to seem good" or "to seem right." The term also means a public decree, an order, or a judgment rendered with great authority.

During the early Christian centuries the term dogma referred to either a particular Christian belief or the sum total of all Christian beliefs and practices. In later years it was more widely understood that Catholic dogmas are, strictly speaking, authoritative church teachings that center on truths divinely revealed to the followers of Christ. Because dogmatic teachings are very important to Catholic life and valid in every age, Pius XII warned church members to fully accept dogmas that have been formulated by the church. In 1978 Pope Paul VI urged Catholics to assent to these great truths in order to be correct in faith.

A dogma is, in fact, a doctrine of the church, yet as an official church teaching it bears greater authority than any single Catholic doctrine. To fully comprehend a dogmatic statement, teachers and students of Catholicism are urged to find out just what the writers of the dogma intended to express and to understand the precise meanings of the words used in stating dogmatic formulas. Even though dogmas of the church are considered infallible (incapable of being in error), in the future some church dogmas may be worded more aptly, using contemporary terminology. They may even be expressed in newer ways in order that Catholics might better understand these important truths and follow them more faithfully.

Dogmas are pronounced by the magisterium of the church and propose truths, revealed by God, which Catholics must believe in order to be saved. Dogmas may be defined and taught by the pope and all the bishops of the church, in unity and harmony, or may be put forth by the holy father alone when he teaches and speaks *ex cathedra* (infallibly, from the "chair of Peter"). Dogmas are based upon scripture and the sacred tradition of the church. Those who deliberately deny particular dogmas are called heretics. The dogmas of the Catholic faith include the Trinity, the Incarnation of Jesus, the Immaculate Conception, the Assumption of Mary, and the real presence in the eucharist. (See also Doctrine, Infallibility, Magisterium.)

EASTER   is the feast on which Catholics and other Christian people celebrate Jesus Christ's rising from death to new life. Belief about the great Easter event, the resurrection of Jesus, is most important to Catholics. It is a sign that sin and death can be overcome, and that all people have the opportunity to be happy with God forever in heaven.

During the first centuries after Christ, there was debate among some church leaders about a proper date for the Easter feast. In 190 Pope Victor I taught that it must be celebrated on a Sunday. In 325 the Council of Nicaea declared that Easter must be held on the first Sunday after the first full moon of springtime. The entire Roman Catholic Church, though, did not accept this method of dating for Easter until the 7th century. Easter Sunday remains a moveable feast that is celebrated on a Sunday between March 22nd and April 25th.

Easter is a very happy, hope-filled time because Jesus, raised from death just as he promised, offers salvation to all humanity. The Mass of the vigil, the night before Easter, is an excellent time for converts to receive the sacraments of initiation—baptism, confirmation, and eucharist. It is also a time when all faithful Catholics renew their baptismal promises.

Easter is the greatest and most joyful feast of the church year. The church's observance of Eastertide lasts for 50 days, beginning on Easter Sunday and ending on Pentecost Sunday. The octave of the easter season begins with the vigil Mass celebrated on the evening before Easter. This octave continues for eight days. The Easter Mass is meant to teach about and celebrate Jesus' resurrection in glory. It celebrates freedom from sin through God's grace, which is received in the sacrament of baptism. (See also Holy Week, Liturgical Year, Resurrection.)

EASTER DUTY   is the name given the church rule that requires Catholics to receive Holy Communion at least once a year, between the first Sunday of Lent and Trinity Sunday, which is one week after Pentecost.

The 4th Lateran Council, under Pope Innocent III in 1215, taught that once-a-year Communion was necessary for all persons who had reached the "age of reason" (about seven years old). For decades the church taught that a person could not enter a church nor receive Christian burial if the Easter Duty was missed. In the 16th century Catholics received communion about three times a year: at Christmas, Easter, and Pentecost.

Since 1551 the church has stressed that Catholics ought to receive the eucharist often. Saint Robert Bellarmine was a great church leader who urged this practice. In 1905 Pius X wrote that daily communion was good for all Catholics.

During the 1960s Vatican Council II taught that Catholics should celebrate every Mass as a holy meal or banquet at which members of the church share the eucharist as their special spiritual food and drink. Paul VI, in March of 1968, noted that the Easter Duty rule is no longer kept by a large number of modern Catholics. He added that receiving communion is important because it helps Catholics keep their lives centered on religious beliefs and hopes. Some church leaders call those who miss the Easter Duty "non-practicing Catholics." (See also Church, Laws of; Easter; Eucharist.)

ECCLESIOLOGY   is the study of the nature, the meaning, the mission, and the structure of the Catholic Church. The term ecclesiology can be traced to the Greek word *ekklesia*, which refers to a "gathering of believers."

Early Christian leaders (Paul, Augustine, and others) viewed the church as a community of faith, the body of Christ or the mystical body of Christ, with the risen Jesus is its head. As the centuries passed however, the church was described more as a visible structure or society, taught and run mainly by a hierarchy of leaders. This view dominated during the 17th, 18th, and 19th centuries. In all probability it helped lead to Vatican I's dogmatic declaration on papal infallibility. In 1943 Pope Pius XII officially stated that Catholics ought to return to thinking about the church of Jesus Christ as his mystical body as well as a visible, earthly society.

Vatican Council II emphasized that the church is the people of God (in addition to being the mystical body). The church is also a community of true believers who should nonetheless examine closely ways to broaden relationships with other Christian and non-Christian religions.

The church must remain a visible society but it should be one that relies on an interior spirituality shared by all its members. The church has four basic marks or traits: 1) it is *one* in faith; 2) it is *holy*—as Jesus Christ the founder of the Christian community is holy; 3) it is *catholic* or universal; and 4) it is *apostolic*, since it is a true continuation of the apostolic community and is dedicated to the mission of preaching and teaching the gospel of Jesus, as were the original apostles of the Lord. (See also Church, Images of; Community; People of God.)

ECUMENISM   (also frequently referred to as the ecumenical movement), is the joint effort by the Catholic Church and other Christian churches to work toward full unity among all Christian peoples. In recent decades the leadership of the church has spoken about overcoming basic differences and obstacles to full unity that now exist between Catholics and other Christian believers. The church invites all of its members to strive to overcome and resolve these problems.

The major Protestant thrust toward ecumenism started in 1910 at a meeting in Edinburgh, Scotland. The World Council of Churches was founded in 1949 and has helped to further this movement. In 1964 Catholic leaders attending Vatican Council II issued the landmark document, *Decree On Ecumenism*, which outlined basic attitudes that Catholics should have toward the ecumenical movement. It also indicated some ways in which Catholics can work for ecumenical unity.

Renewal of the church and a willingness on the part of all active Catholics to witness to Christ's teaching are crucial to the development of Christian unity. Prayers for unity are also essential if the movement is to succeed. Ecumenical prayer services attended by members of various Christian denominations, are encouraged by church leaders.

The church requests that Catholics join other Christians in projects for social good. Leaders also call for dialogue among the experts of various denominations so that complete unity and acceptance might result. Catholics should respect and recognize the special gifts and God-given talents enjoyed by non-Catholic Christians. They should be willing to openly and honestly discuss ways to cooperate with other Christian believers, and seek the reform and constant renewal of the Catholic Church, which will contribute to the full unity of all Christians.

Note of Interest: Pope John XXIII founded the Secretariat for Promoting Christian Unity in 1960. This Roman Curia bureau is working to create deeper, more open, more complete relationships with other Christians. The Catholic Church is not a formal member of the World Council of Churches, but it does send representatives and observers to meetings held by this organization. John Paul II has recently prayed for full communion among Christians. He has stated that the ecumenical effort is a priority imposed on our actions that is based on God's will. (See also Christian Unity Week, Ecclesiology.)

ENCYCLICALS are formal letters or messages written by popes to all members of the Catholic Church. These letters offer guidelines on matters of faith, morality, and Christian discipline.

The first encyclical was issued by Pope Benedict XIV in 1740 and was titled *Ubi Primum*. It addressed the important duties of church leaders. Sending out encyclicals to Catholics around the world became a common practice with Pius IX in the 19th century, and it has continued ever since.

The titles of the encyclical letters usually come from the first few words of the text. Because these messages are issued by the leader of the church, Catholics are instructed to accept the teachings they contain. Yet not all encyclicals are meant to be infallible statements. Many official teachings from encyclicals will be updated, restated, or more perfectly phrased in the future. Encyclical teachings do have special authority which all Catholics should recognize and honor.

The church affirms that the pope is the primary head and true pastor of all church members. It is in this capacity that he issues his teachings and opinions in encyclical letters. There have been some encyclicals written for limited areas and persons and not for the entire church. These specialized encyclicals are referred to as encyclical epistles. Since the time of Leo XIII (1878), about 150 official encyclicals and special encyclical epistles have been published. The most recent have been John Paul II's *Redemptor Hominis*, *Dives In Miserecordia*, and *Laborem Exercens*; Paul VI's *Humanae Vitae*; and John XXIII's *Mater Et Magistra* and *Pacem In Terris*. (See also Magisterium, Pope.)

EPIPHANY is a solemn church feast on which Catholics celebrate the manifestation of the divinity of the Lord Jesus. This feast has traditionally been celebrated on January 6th. One of the events commemorated on Epiphany is the visit by the Magi (or wise men) to the newborn savior (Mt 2:1–12).

The Epiphany, first celebrated in the 3rd century, was noted in writings by Clement of Alexandria. This popular feast soon spread to all parts of the Christian world. By the Middle Ages it was a custom in some places to bless the homes of Christians on Epiphany. Part of this ceremony was the inscription (with chalk) of the names of the Magi; Melchior, Balthasar, and Caspar, above the doors of Christian homes.

The feast of Epiphany also celebrates the birth of Jesus and his baptism at the beginning of his public ministry. Some members of religious orders renew their personal vows of poverty, chastity, and obedience on Epiphany.

In many countries January 6th is the only date on which the feast of the Epiphany is celebrated. In the United States, however, it is celebrated on the second Sunday after Christmas. The Epiphany is one of the most ancient and most important of Christian feasts. In some areas of the world this feast coincides with twelfth night parties and festivities. (See also Christmas, Liturgical Year.)

EPISTLE　　means "letter." The New Testament letters, which carry the names of Paul, John, Peter, and James as "authors," are commonly called epistles. The word *epistle* is still used sometimes to indicate the first or the first and second readings from the bible during Mass. The Latin *epistola* and the Greek *epistole* both mean "letter" or "message."

Twenty-one books of the New Testament are epistles. They were written to early Christian communities and individuals to instruct them about basic beliefs and proper moral behavior. They offer practical advice for strengthening faith, and they dispute false doctrines. Fourteen epistles are attributed to Paul, though current research suggests that Paul himself did not actually compose all fourteen letters.

Most likely Paul did write the epistle to the Romans, 1 and 2 Corinthians, the epistles to the Galatians, Philippians, to Philemon, and also the first letter to the Thessalonians. Recent research casts doubt on his actual authorship of the epistles to the Colossians and the Ephesians, as well as the second letter to the Thessalonians. Persons other than Paul wrote the epistles to the Hebrews, 1 and 2 Timothy, and Titus. These latter epistles are "pauline" in style and intent. The authors were working within the same early church as Paul and were noticeably influenced by his remarkable preaching and teaching.

There are seven additional epistles in the New Testament. These are the epistle of James, 1 and 2 Peter, the epistle of Jude, and 1, 2, and 3 John. Although attributed to these apostles of Jesus, they were probably written by Christians who were their close followers. (See also Bible, Books of; Inspiration; New Testament; Paul.)

ESTHER   was a Jewish heroine who saved the Hebrew people from destruction in Persia. The name Esther is probably a form of the Persian word *stareh*, which means star.

The book of Esther is in the Old Testament. It is a ten-chapter story describing how Esther became the Queen of King Xerxes I of Persia in 470 B.C. A secret plan to kill Xerxes was foiled by Esther (with a little aid from her Uncle Mordecai), and the grateful king allowed the Hebrews to fight and thus defeat all of their enemies in a two-day battle. This great victory is remembered on the Jewish feast of Purim.

The story of Esther was written around 100 B.C., and may well be a novel written to show that God saves his people from evil. It may also have been written in an attempt to build a strong sense of nationalism and spirit among the Jews. Some biblical scholars believe that the book of Esther is based on an ancient Babylonian myth. It could also be a retelling of a story by the Greek writer Herodotus. This book was not among the Old Testament texts found in the Qumran (Dead Sea Scroll) caves.

Saint Jerome placed the *Book of Esther* in his Latin version of scripture (the *Vulgate*), but he was concerned that the work was not pure history. The Council of Trent taught in the 16th century that the book of Esther does belong in the bible. Esther's unique story shows how much God cares for his chosen people and how he works through the words and deeds of both men and women. (See also Bible, Books of; Dead Sea Scrolls.)

EUCHARIST   is one of the seven sacraments of the church, but the word eucharist is also used as a synonym for the Catholic liturgical communal action called the Mass. The word comes from the Greek *eucharistia*, which means "thanksgiving." Catholics maintain that Jesus Christ is fully and truly present in the eucharist, in the forms of bread and wine, and that the eucharistic celebration is the central act of worship and community for all believers. The holy eucharist is the essential spiritual food and drink — the spiritual nourishment — of church members.

The eucharistic celebration, the Mass, has roots in the Hebrew *seder*, a ritual meal commemorating the Passover and exodus. It was in the setting of a Passover meal that Jesus, in the company of His apostles, instituted the eucharist (at the Last Supper). He blessed and shared bread with them saying, "Take this and eat it, this is my body," He blessed and shared wine with them saying, "All of you must drink from it, for this is my blood." He then commanded his followers to celebrate the eucharist in his name and memory (Mt 26:26-29, Lk 22:17-20).

Through the first few centuries of community-life, the church celebrated the eucharist on Sundays always as well as on a few other special occasions. It was celebrated as a meal. In the 2nd and 3rd centuries the concept of Mass as a sharing-meal gradually diminished. The eucharistic prayer (the canon), and the formal consecration of the bread and wine into the body and blood of Christ became central features. The Fourth Lateran Council (1215) defined "transubstantiation," as the proper term for the process of bringing about the mystery of the *real presence.* In recent years other more comprehensible terms have been used to describe the real presence of Christ in the eucharist. But in the 1965 encyclical *Mysterium Fidei,* Paul VI stressed that transubstantiation is the preferred term for describing the change from bread and wine to the body and blood of Christ.

Vatican Council II invited Catholics to an awareness of the real presence of Jesus in the *community of believers* assembled for the eucharist. The eucharist should transform the worshipping community into a body, a united people, who live, act, hope, and dream as a truly converted, committed Christian group. It is still emphasized that the Mass is a sacrifice, the eucharist a sacrament, yet the celebration is a sharing-meal that unites believers and helps them—through frequent reception of communion—to become followers of Christ (see Jn 6:47-58, and Vatican II's *Constitution on the Sacred Liturgy*).

The church teaches that only priests and bishops may preside at the Mass and consecrate the eucharist. Other church members may take part in the eucharistic liturgy as lectors, commentators, special ministers (or extraordinary ministers) of the eucharist, deacons, music ministers, ushers and planners. The official church stresses that the eucharist is necessary for salvation, and that the Mass is indeed a sacrifice and a meal, and that Jesus Christ is fully and really present in the consecrated bread and wine. These doctrines have been stated or restated by the Trent, Constance, and Fourth Lateran Councils, and by Paul VI in his 1965 eucharist encyclical.

Note of Interest: The Catholic Church rules that members must receive the eucharist at least once a year. For more information, see Easter Duty. To receive at any time one must be in the state of grace, and not in the state of mortal sin. All are expected to fast—no food or liquids (besides water), may be taken within one hour prior to receiving communion. (See also Liturgy of the Word/Eucharist, Sacrament, Worship.)

EUTHANASIA is the act or practice of killing individuals (or or allowing them to die by not following normal medical procedures) who are hopelessly sick or injured.

It is often referred to as mercy killing. Catholics are warned that euthanasia is really murder.

Two important themes emerge in any serious discussion of euthanasia: 1) All Christians should maintain great respect for human life and avoid all actions that might destroy it. 2) Only God is the creator of life and all human beings have special worth and dignity provided by him.

Current debate centering on acts of euthanasia revolves around the idea of putting people to death as compared to letting them die. Purposely putting someone to death—by suffocation or through an overdose of drugs, for example—is an act of murder. (It's not necessary, however, to use extraordinary means simply to prolong life). Giving powerful drugs to suffering patients, to ease severe pain even if these drugs may shorten life is permissible in some cases. This whole matter is very complex however, and church leaders recognize that official teaching on the matter of euthanasia may be refined and/or made more definite in the future.

The church's current official position on acts of euthanasia has been more clearly developed since Vatican II. For euthanasia to take place there must be an intentional act that is directly opposed to life. Acts of euthanasia do great dishonor to the creator of all life forms. All human beings should try to search for ways to safeguard and respect the lives of others. (See also Commandments of God, Death/Dying, Morality.)

EVANGELIZATION is the proclamation of the good news that Jesus Christ offers eternal salvation to all members of the human race. Evangelization is the foremost duty or mission of all faithful members of the Catholic Church.

Vatican Council II taught that evangelization occurs when persons who have never heard (or persons who are no longer active Christians) *actually hear* the good news of the gospel. In 1975 Pope Paul VI wrote a statement called *Evangelii Nuntiandi* that stressed the need for a renewed willingness to preach and share the good news with others. Two years later the American bishops opened an office of evangelization to minister to the needs of the 12 million inactive Catholics in the United States. During 1979 the bishops undertook a study to find out if Catholics really believed that the good news of the Gospel touched all aspects of their daily lives.

It is important for Catholics—including all lay persons—to actively witness to the gospel and to recognize as the people of God that they have an essential mission and duty to proclaim the gospel message. This should be done through words, work, and Christian lifestyles.

In 1979 Pope John Paul II taught that evangelization is above all the announcement of the good word of Christ the Savior who offers salvation to humankind. Most programs of evangelizing in Catholic parishes center on visiting homes of fallen-away or potential Catholics and on adult education or bible-study meetings. The church, following the lead of Vatican II, teaches that local bishops ought to support the work done by Christian missions, and that notable increases in activity by lay persons and vocations to religious life are needed for effective evangelization. (See also Gospel, Mission, Witness.)

EXORCISM is the driving out of evil spirits from possessed persons. An exorcist is the individual who performs the exorcism. Both of these terms come from the Greek *exorkizein* which means to drive away by command. The exorcism rite of the Catholic Church includes prayers and forceful commands demanding that evil spirits (or devils and demons) leave the person possessed and stop injuring him or her.

It is reported in the New Testament that Jesus powerfully commanded many demons to leave suffering people (see especially the Gospel of Mark). Church tradition holds that the devil—the power of evil and darkness—is very real and is humankind's great enemy (or adversary). He is opposed to goodness and the spiritual well-being of men and women. Yet, humankind has once and for all been redeemed by Christ through his death and resurrection. Sin and evil's power have been conquered by him. For centuries exorcist was one of the minor orders received by all men preparing for the Catholic priesthood. The official church declared in 1972 that the minor order of exorcist, as well as some other minor orders, would no longer be received.

Modern scholars maintain that many cases of possession are actually caused by pathological (natural) factors rather than by the supernatural power of evil spirits. Official church exorcisms are very rare but those which are performed are usually administered by priests who are the special delegates of their local bishops. Church leaders recognize and believe that a person is truly possessed by supernatural evil only if there is no natural explanation for the problems the possessed person is experiencing.

A church exorcism includes prayers for the one possessed and the use of sacramentals such as holy water and the crucifix. In the sacrament of baptism, the church calls upon the person baptized to reject the devil and all that is opposed to goodness. The baptism ceremony contains exorcism prayers for protection of those to be baptized from evil's power. The *Rite of Christian Initiation of Adults* contains prayers for the convert, praying that he or she may remain free from sin and evil and be always preserved from the influence of the devil. (See also Baptism, Catechumenate and the RCIA, Prayer.)

EXTRAORDINARY MINISTERS are unordained persons who receive special permission to distribute holy communion. They often receive this right because there are not enough priests and deacons to perform this ministry. Extraordinary ministers may be religious or laypersons.

In the early church lay people gave the eucharist to others as well as to themselves until the 8th century. This practice declined as emphasis on the divine presence in the eucharist increased. The canon law of the church was updated in 1966 to allow local church leaders to use extraordinary ministers. By 1971 bishops were commissioning extraordinary ministers of the eucharist. In January of 1973 the Vatican offered guidelines for the selection and approval of these special ministers.

The church often experiences a pressing need for extraordinary ministers in large parishes in places where there are numerous sick and older people who can only receive the sacrament in their homes. With the view that all baptized persons are priestly members of the church, the Vatican has issued a rite or ceremony for commissioning lay and religious ministers of the eucharist. This rite offers men and women a sacred blessing for their ministry.

The bishop of a diocese is usually the one who grants permission to individuals who wish to perform this special ministry. In certain cases, and in times of great need, priests may appoint persons to be extraordinary ministers for a limited period of time. All of these special ministers should receive the rite of institution through the commissioning ritual mentioned above.

Note of Interest: The Vatican stated in 1978 that the term "Special Ministers of Holy Communion" is more accurate and should be used instead of "Extraordinary Ministers." This newer terminology is incorporated in the rite of institution. (See also Eucharist, Lay Ministries.)

EZEKIEL was a priest and prophet who is called the third major Hebrew prophet of the Old Testament. He made his prophecies from 593 to 571 B.C. while the Hebrews were captive exiles in Babylonia. Ezekiel warned the people to avoid all sins, to be faithful to Yahweh (God) instead of the Babylonian gods, and to have hope for a new Israel once they were set free.

The book of Ezekiel in the bible contains 48 chapters. The first section forsees the destruction of the city of Jerusalem. Later chapters (40-48) center on the hope for freedom and a perfect religious and political life for the Hebrews. The book reports many visions seen by the prophet, such as "God's chariot" in Chapter 1 and the "dry bones" of Chapter 37. It also tells about his symbolic actions, such as eating a paper scroll and shaving his head. Some students of the bible believe that Ezekiel may have written only some of this book. They believe that many skilled authors added to his writings over the years.

Catholic scholars have noted that Ezekiel's visions could in some cases be retold dreams or products of his imagination. They do stress that Ezekiel's message was pinpointed on the glory and divinity of God plus each person's responsibility for his or her sins. They suspect that the vivid imagery found in Ezekiel aided the persons who put together the Book of Revelation in the New Testament. (See also Bible, Books of; Prophet.)

FAITH is one of the three theological virtues (the others are hope and charity). Faith may be defined as trust, conviction, commitment to and belief in the God who reveals himself to humankind. Some people use the word to mean "the faith," referring to belief in the essential teachings and doctrines of the church. The word faith comes from the Latin *fides*, which means belief.

The New Testament indicates that Jesus, who was the promised messiah and God's greatest revelation, expected his followers to have faith in him and his good news about salvation. The belief of the early church centered on Jesus' death and resurrection and the importance of these saving events for the whole of humanity. Great thinkers like Augustine and Thomas Aquinas have held that true faith is like an inner light, a thorough conviction. The official church strongly emphasized faith as an act of the intellect to offset the influences of the Protestant Reformation

(16th century and beyond). Some theologians continue to explain faith, at least in part, as an intellectual act of assent to divine truths, under the influence of the person's will moved by God's grace.

Faith is indeed a gift from God, a conviction (and, in a sense, a willingness to risk) that God is really disclosing himself to the world. It is conviction that Jesus is the Lord and savior of all, and that through trust in God a great, dynamic friendship between the divine and the human is deepened. Some theologians stress that faith is communal as well as personal, that the gift of faith helps individuals share in the faith of the entire people of God, the church. The light of faith in each believer helps him or her to accept Jesus as Lord and to grow, day-by-day, into deeper, more mature, faith-filled relationships with God and others.

Vatican Council II taught that faith must be a free response, that individuals must freely choose to commit themselves to God and the kingdom now being built. Therefore no one should be forced to believe. Through the help of the Spirit men and women can accept God's self-disclosure (revelation) with greater ease, find him always and everywhere, and seek his will for humanity. The council stressed that all faithful Christians should give witness to the whole world to total trust in God, and thereby show the common hope and the love shared by believers.

The council added that in faith "man (and woman) entrusts (the) whole self freely to God, offering 'the full submission of intellect and will to God who reveals,' and freely assenting to the truth revealed by him" (*Dei Verbum*, n. 5). (See also Atheism, Free Will, Virtues.)

FAMILY MINISTRY   is the call to families (the domestic church), to share the good news of Jesus Christ, to worship as a body with the church community, to reflect with, teach (catechize), and unselfishly serve one another. In so doing family members become better prepared to be living witnesses to Jesus in the world, ready and willing to evangelize all those outside the immediate family circle and to worship with, teach, and serve constantly the entire people of God. The bishops of the church have stressed that family ministry must remain a major priority for Catholic Christians in order to enrich the lives of sound families and to assist and help heal the pains of hurting families.

Christianity is a way of life to be passed on and shared freely with others. The followers of Jesus are called to love and depend upon one another. During recent decades the modern family has become more and more fragmented and isolated from others.

Some cultural shifts reinforce this: increase in divorce rates, both husbands and wives working, more unwed mothers, experimental marriages, prevalency of birth control. Recognizing all of this, the international Synod of Bishops met in 1980 to consider the role of the Christian family in the modern world. The synod proposed a charter on family rights, which advised families to 1) live in contradiction to the strains of modern culture; 2) be critical of injustice and disregard for spiritual values; 3) affirm that valid marriages cannot be dissolved and hold to the teachings of *Humanae Vitae*; and 4) live as a true domestic church, promoting growth in holiness through faith, hope, and charity.

The belief that parents are the first and foremost educators of their children has received renewed attention because of Vatican Council II (see especially n.3 of the council's *Declaration on Christian Education*). The official church seeks to offer support to mothers and fathers who must fill this important role. A number of Catholic parishes now sponsor family-centered catechesis programs that encourage families to learn, pray, and celebrate together. These programs also help prepare them—as baptized members of the people of God—to live and serve as humble Christians in their homes and in the wider circle of human and secular life.

In May 1978 the American bishops expressed a continuing interest and concern for authentic ministry to modern families by issuing a *Pastoral Plan of Action for Family Ministry*. They called for renewed efforts in the planning and carrying out of effective ministry programs that meet the human needs and hopes of families. Such programs should include active listening to families, the enablement and training of family ministers, and encouragement of family members who seek to minister to each other. In seeking to better evangelize and catechize modern families, the church hopes to acquire more research data on the countless factors that influence, even hinder, healthy family living. And the church continues to urge families to share the gospel message in the home, to pray as a community, to teach one another kindly, and also to take the good news of Christ into the world to humbly serve other human beings. (See also Divorce, Matrimony, Ministry.)

FASTING   is the practice of doing without eating solid foods for designated periods of time. Catholics in the United States who are between 21 and 59 years of age must fast on two days; Ash Wednesday and Good Friday. This means that church members may eat only one full meal and two small meals on these days.

Abstinence is not the same as fasting. To abstain means to not eat meat or meat-products on certain days. The church expects its members to abstain—if they are 14 years and older—on Ash Wednesday, Good Friday, and all of the Fridays during Lent.

The bible reveals that Jesus Christ and the apostles fasted at times. Church history indicates that Christians often fasted on Wednesdays and Fridays, and did not eat meat on Fridays. They did these things to remember and honor the sufferings and death of Jesus and to do penance for sins. For years United States Catholics fasted on all lenten days (except Sundays) and on some days before important feast as Christmas and the Assumption. In 1966 Pope Paul relaxed many of these very strict Catholic fasting laws.

Fasting is a practice that helps persons to grow spiritually. It is best done when it is linked with special acts of charity and daily prayer. Although meat may now be eaten on most Fridays of the year, abstinence is still a practice that is encouraged and promoted by church leaders.

The American bishops agreed in 1974 that Ash Wednesday, Good Friday, and lenten Fridays should be held as days of fast and abstinence. The teaching church continues to urge all Catholics to choose on their own to fast, even though many of the stricter fasting laws have been relaxed. (See also Lent.)

FATHERS AND DOCTORS OF THE CHURCH were outstanding leaders, writers, and teachers during the earlier centuries of the church. The titles Fathers of the Church and Doctors of the Church do not mean exactly the same thing, but the official Fathers and Doctors do share some similar qualifications and traits. Both titles refer to spiritual persons who were church writers and theologians, and both refer to persons who were living witnesses to the gospel of Jesus.

Four criteria are used to establish someone as an authentic Father of the Church. He must be: 1) a teacher of correct doctrine; 2) one who lives a holy lifestyle; 3) approved by the official Catholic Church; and 4) linked to antiquity—the earliest centuries of the Christian community. The Patristic Age extends from the 1st and 2nd centuries up to and including the 8th century. The persons often associated with the earliest Christian literary and faith-dynamic period of church life are called Apostolic Fathers (a term coined during the 17th century), indicating some kind of contact between these fathers and the apostles or their immediate followers. Apostolic Fathers include: Clement of Rome, Ignatius of Antioch, Polycarp, Papias, Justin Martyr, Irenaeus, and Clement of Alexandria. The later Church Fathers include Ambrose, Augustine, Jerome, Athanasius, Gregory the Great, Basil the Great, Gregory of Nazianzen, and John Chrysostom. The last of the great fathers were Gregory the Great and Isidore of Seville in the Western Church, and John of Damascus, in the Eastern Church.

Doctors of the Church meet the identical criteria, but do not have to have a close link with Christian antiquity. The Doctors were learned and holy individuals, most of whom were teachers of Christian doctrine. Doctors of the Church are so named by an explicit council statement or by a papal decree. There are now 32 recognized Doctors of the Church, and some of these are also official Church Fathers. The latest Doctors are Teresa of Avila and Catherine of Siena named by Paul VI in 1970. These two are the first women to be named Doctors of the Church.

The Doctors of the Church include: Albert the Great, Alphonsus Liguori, Ambrose—also a Father of the Church, Anselm, Anthony of Padua, Athanasius—also a Father, Augustine—also a Father, Basil the Great—also a Father, Bede the Venerable, Bernard of Clairvaux, Bonaventure, Catherine of Siena, Cyril of Alexandria—also a Father, Cyril of Jerusalem—also a Father, Ephraim—also a Father, Francis de Sales, Gregory of Nazianzen—also a Father, Gregory the Great—also a Father, Hilary of Poitiers—also a Father, Isidore of Seville—also a Father, Jerome—also a Father, John Chrysostom—also a Father, John of Damascus—also a Father, John of the Cross, Lawrence of Brindisi, Leo the Great—also a Father, Peter Canisius, Peter Chrysologus—also a Father, Peter Damian, Robert Bellarmine, Teresa of Avila, Thomas Aquinas. (See also Doctrine; Saints, Communion of; Theology.)

FORTY HOURS DEVOTION is a form of worship that gives members of Catholic parishes a special chance to honor, adore, and pray to Jesus Christ in the blessed sacrament—the eucharist. Forty Hours is usually held in parishes once a year and begins with holy Mass. A large eucharistic host is placed in a gold container called a monstrance which is carried through the parish church in procession by a priest. This part of 40 Hours closes when the priest places the blessed sacrament on the alter for all to see and visit during the 40 Hours. To close this ceremony several prayers are said and hymns are sung. A mass of "reposition," 40 hours later, concludes the 40 Hours devotion.

This practice developed during the 14th century. It was first held in Milan, Italy in 1527. Pope Clement VIII decreed in 1592 that it was to be held in all parishes in Rome. This custom then spread to other parts of the world.

The number of hours is "forty" since it is believed that Jesus' body was in the tomb that long before the resurrection on Easter Sunday. The main reasons for holding Forty Hours were: 1) to give Catholics a chance to pray for protection against troubles, and 2) to allow time to make amends and do penances for sins.

In this century Forty Hours has been devoted to the adoration of Jesus in the blessed sacrament rather than making amends for faults. In 1973 the church decreed that the devotion should take place once a year in parishes and that Catholics should spend periods of time during the 40 hours thinking about the mystery of eucharist and adoring the Lord. (See also Benediction, Eucharist, Worship.)

FREE WILL/RELIGIOUS FREEDOM is the capacity to be responsible for one's own decisions and actions. In exercising free will, people make choices (voluntarily and freely) for good or evil. The concept of free will is at the foundation of all Christian morality and points to the essential dignity and uniqueness of every human person.

The idea that all people enjoy the freedom to make choices appeared in the writings of many of the Fathers of the Church (Augustine in particular). The church teaches that to do God's will and to achieve full union with him involves free will and God's gift of grace. To freely work toward salvation and to seek God in everyday life is a loving, mature response to God's unmerited gift of divine grace.

Vatican Council II maintained (with regard to religious freedom and liberty) that every human person has a right to religious freedom, adding that this special freedom is based upon the authentic dignity of each man and woman and is in accord with God's divine revelation. Vatican II also taught that nations and governments should recognize religious freedom as a civil right for everyone. Individuals deserve religious freedom and groups of individuals—when they act in community for proper goals and reasons—should also be accorded religious liberty.

For a complete study of Vatican II's teaching on this, see the *Declaration on Religious Freedom*. (See also Faith, Grace, Morality.)

FRUITS OF THE SPIRIT   named by Saint Paul in Galatians 5, enable Christians to live in humble, unselfish ways. These fruits are: charity, joy, peace, patience, gentleness, goodness, mildness, faith, endurance, modesty, self-control, and chastity.

The fruits of the Spirit are gifts from God. Paul lists some of the evil effects that persons experience when they are not guided by the Spirit: lewd behavior, impure living, worshipping false gods, sorcery, hostility, frequent arguments, jealousies, rage and anger, selfishness, dissension, envy, drunken behavior, and sexual misconduct.

Catholics who are always open to these fruits from God's Spirit will grow and mature as faithful Christians. (See also Holiness, Trinity.)

GIFTS OF THE SPIRIT   are seven unique gifts provided by the Holy Spirit. The seven gifts are given to persons in the sacrament of baptism and are strengthened with the reception of confirmation.

The seven gifts help Catholics lead grace-filled, moral lives. They are listed in Isaiah, 11:2-3: 1) Wisdom—bestows the ability to judge God's will for us. 2) Understanding—helps us to know what God has revealed. 3) Knowledge—aids us in knowing things as they really are. 4) Fortitude—provides the strength and courage needed to face troubles. 5) Counsel—the gift that helps us decide what to do in problem situations. 6) Piety—helps us reverently approach God as loving father. 7) Fear of the Lord—teaches us that God is absolutely above us and deserving of our utter reverence, awe, and adoration, while remaining friend and Father. The number seven is often used in the bible to indicate perfection, fullness, or completion. (See also Baptism, Confirmation, Trinity.)

GODPARENTS   are those persons who ask, along with the natural parents, for the Christian baptism of a child. Ideally there are to be two godparents present at each baptism—one male, one female—and both should be practicing Catholics. In special cases there may be one Catholic godparent present and one non-Catholic who serves as a witness to the baptism. The godparents of a child accept the important role of caring for the young person's on-going spiritual welfare if the child's parents cannot do so.

In order to become a godparent, a Catholic should be at least 14 years old, already baptized and confirmed, be accepted by the child's natural parents as a valid godparent, and be fully willing to assume the rather important role that godparents must play in the lives of their god-children.

Godparents represent the whole Christian community of faith and promise the love and support of this community to the newly baptized child. The role of godparents during the actual baptism ceremony though important, is secondary to that of the natural parents.

Godparents are asked to offer wise advice, assistance, and a wholesome upbringing for the child when the natural parents cannot. During the baptismal ceremony, the church's official minister asks godparents to profess their Catholic beliefs and to be ready to share these through word and example with their godchild. It is recommended that godparents take part in formal instructions and meetings that will help them prepare, along with the parents, for the actual baptism ceremony.

Note of Interest: In the case of the baptism and confirmation of an older person (adult or teenager), no godparents participate in the celebration. One older person of the same sex as the candidate, a practicing and baptized Catholic, is present at the ceremony as a sponsor. This sponsor is called by the church to be an example of Christian living for the convert at all times. (See also Baptism.)

GOSPEL   refers to the good news of salvation brought to humankind by Jesus Christ, the son of God. Gospel derives from the Anglo-Saxon *godspell*, which means "god story." While there is only one gospel there are four written versions of the good news in the New Testament.

The writers of the four gospels—often referred to as evangelists—were not attempting to write a complete biography of Jesus' life. Rather they wrote about significant events and sayings to show that salvation comes to men and women through Jesus' saving works. At the heart of each version of the gospel is the death and resurrection of Jesus.

The word gospel can mean any one of these three things: 1) the entire ministry and teachings of Jesus; 2) one of the four versions of the good news written by the evangelists; 3) the reading of part of one of the four gospel versions during a Catholic Mass or other liturgy.

All four gospels were written between 65 and 100. It is believed that the book of Mark was the first to be written, then Matthew, Luke, and John, in that order. (See also Evangelization, New Testament, Synoptics.)

GRACE is God's free, unmerited, loving gift of his own life and presence to people. Through a loving and open response to this gift, persons are transformed and share in God's life and love. They become more and more like Jesus Christ. For a person to gain eternal salvation, he or she must enjoy the grace of God. The word grace derives from the Latin *gratia*, which means "favor" and "free gift."

Human beings receive grace as a totally free gift, through Christ's saving works, and this gift transforms (or elevates) human nature to a newer, higher level of existence. In the New Testament this grace is presented as *the* principle of Christian living in that it impels the followers of Jesus to be more like him, to do good works, and to act righteously. Since the beginning the church community has been plagued by heresies and misunderstandings about grace. Augustine pointed out that it is an unmerited gift. The church of the Middle Ages struggled with false teachings on predestination and stated that grace and salvation are meant for all persons, not simply a chosen few. By the time of the Council of Trent (16th century), it was taught that, through this powerful gift from God, people are transformed interiorly by God's own Spirit.

The question of how men and women remain free beings, even as they receive God's self-communication of life and love, is posed and studied today by numerous theologians. Grace is really the gift of God's Spirit and so can change people for the better if they seek to develop a deeper, ongoing relationship with God and seek likewise to avoid sin. Grace is God's gratuitous love given to humans. It is not a "thing" to be measured or quantified.

Vatican Council II noted that the Spirit of God dwells in people, and in the church community through the gift of grace. God makes a free and loving offer of his own life to all persons in order that they be saved. The loving relationship between God and those who lovingly respond to his gift is deepened, day by day, through prayer and works of charity and justice. This loving union is also strengthened through the reception of the seven sacraments, especially the eucharist and reconciliation. Grace is sometimes classified as actual, sanctifying, created, and uncreated. All members of the people of God are called to reflect upon the mystery of grace. (See also Conversion, Faith, Revelation.)

HEAVEN   is that state of being or condition that all enjoy who have gained salvation. Those who exist in heaven enjoy the beatific vision, a complete and perfect happiness with God.

The New Testament speaks of seeing God in the blessedness of life-after-death. This seeing is mentioned in the beatitudes and by Saint Paul who claims that believers will be with God face to face (Mt 5:8; 2 Cor 3:12-18). The first letter of John says that men and women will see God, and indicates that they will be transformed to be like God in heavenly happiness. The New Testament also describes heaven as eternal life. The major teachings of the Catholic Church on heaven include the *Benedictus Deus* by Pope Benedict XII (published in 1336), and some statements by the Council of Florence (1439). These hold that all who die worthy of heaven — and without any need of purgatory — see God clearly and immediately after death. Recently, Pius XII (in 1943) and Paul VI (in 1968) re-emphasized the church's long-standing doctrine on heaven. Some theologians describe heaven as a place from which Jesus came, to which he has returned, and to which all who have gained salvation will go.

Still others stress that heaven should be considered a state of being, a condition full of joy and light rather than as a place (in the geographical sense). Heaven is complete union with God—the antithesis of the loneliness, separation, and loss of hell. Church teachings offer believers a sense of hope. They present heaven as a true goal of human life, and as the unselfish, perfect, and total union with God.

The church also teaches that some persons begin to enjoy heaven right after death, while some endure a period of being purified in purgatory first. The church maintains that each person is judged at the time of death as to whether he or she has accepted and responded to God's gift of grace and life. This judgment is called the particular judgment of every person. At the second coming, all who have lived and are judged worthy of salvation (this is the final judgment) will begin to enjoy the heavenly, perfected kingdom of God and live within the loving community of all who have reached salvation, in the holy presence of God. (See also Hell, Hope, Salvation.)

HEBREWS   is one of the terms used to identify the members of the nation of Israel. Two more common names are Jews and Israelites.

The term Hebrew was most often used in biblical days to refer to those members of the Israelite nation who spoke the Aramaic language and adhered strictly to ancient Jewish customs and laws.

The Hebrews are remembered by catholics and other Christians as the chosen descendants of Abraham who tried to live up to the covenant that had been made between God and his people. This God (Yahweh) is the same unique, one God in whom Catholics believe and to whom they pledge their faith and love. (See also Abraham, People of God, Zionism.)

HELL   is the state or condition of alienation from God for all eternity. The Church teaches that a person's own free, complete, and deliberate choice of sin and evil leads to hell. Hell begins right after death for those who die in sin, and lasts forever.

The term hell does not appear in the Old Testament, yet a roughly equivalent term, *Gehenna*, does appear. Gehenna was an unholy place, an actual spot in ancient Israel where the corpses of those who revolted against Yahweh were thrown. In some older Jewish documents, Gehenna is pictured as a dark and fearsome place, a place of fire where unfortunates are chained and suffering. Gehenna is mentioned again in the New Testament, particularly by Jesus in the gospels. It is depicted as a place of fire where there is pain and tears. The Athanasian Creed, produced by the church in the late 400s, claims that hell — a state of eternal damnation and punishment for sinfulness — truly exists. The church's belief in hell was upheld by the Fourth Lateran Council (1215), Second Council of Lyons (1274), and other councils, and by Pope Benedict XII in 1336. The church has continued to teach that hell is eternal damnation for the sinner. Yet hell was not directly mentioned by Vatican Council II nor discussed by Paul VI in his comprehensive *Credo of The People of God*. Some theologians describe hell as a place of fire and unending punishment and torment.

Some modern thinkers hold that the New Testament *assumes*, but cannot confirm, the existence of a hell. Jesus may have used such dramatic imagery to strongly urge his listeners to turn away from sinfulness and to recognize and accept the kingdom-at-hand. A number of scholars claim that neither Jesus nor anyone else has ever taught, definitively, that a specific human being has been permanently banished to hell. Some writers and thinkers go so far as to suggest that the notion of eternal damnation is just out of the question. Others emphasize that heaven and hell are something like two poles: men and women are free to respond to God's grace (and thus, strive for the pole called heaven) or they can lean freely toward sinfulness and total separation from God and others (and move toward the other pole, hell).

The church stresses that God does not dispatch persons to

hell. Human beings, throughout their lifetimes, either respond to God's gift of grace and gain salvation, or they reject God's free gift and opt for unending existence without God and others. Hell is often pictured as the unspeakable torment of complete loneliness and loss. The church still holds that there is a devil — a powerful adversary of humankind—and that those who die after rejecting totally the gift of grace are judged worthy of hell. The gospel of Matthew, Chapter 25, speaks of a final judgment at the second coming, when all who have lived will be either considered members of God's perfected kingdom or bound to eternity in hell. (See also Free Will, Heaven, Sin.)

HOLINESS is the state of being sanctified and dedicated in a very special way to God. The holy man or woman is one who possesses God's gift of grace and is committed, actively and unselfishly, to love of God, to moral goodness, and to bettering the world for all persons. Catholics state that God is all-perfect and all-holy, that Jesus Christ was holy, and that all church members are called to Christian holiness.

In the Old Testament God speaks of himself as the Holy One (Is 40:25; Jer 50:29). The Hebrew people believed that a truly holy man or woman was someone completely dedicated to serving Yahweh and that the nation of Israel — the nation set apart as God's chosen people — was likewise very holy (Lv 17-26). The Catholic Church affirms that God is infinitely perfect and holy, completely pure and unchangeable, totally separate from evil, the source of all grace, and that he does demand holiness from all members of the human race.

The church also teaches that Jesus Christ is uniquely holy in his love for God and for all peoples. The Son of God calls all men and women to be devoted to the Father and to imitate his own holiness and charity. The church is truly holy, it is a living sign of God and Jesus Christ here on earth, it has been sanctified by Christ, is guided by his Holy Spirit, and has received an important mission from Jesus to proclaim the gospel of salvation, to baptize, and to call all men and women to holiness. Each member of the church is called to holiness through the gift of grace and baptism.

Vatican Council II maintained that Catholic Christians can progress in holiness through prayer, devotions, and the reception of the eucharist. The council also noted that by doing one's life work (and by performing acts of charity as well), in the name of Jesus, a Christian grows in holiness and is better able to cope with trials, troubles, and problems. Those Catholics (whether clergy, religious, or laity) who practice the evangelical counsels of poverty, chastity, and obedience are considered outstanding witnesses to and examples of holiness. Catholics hold that all church members have the duty to work together in harmony to make the entire church more holy and a more perfect sign of Christ in this world.

Note of Interest: Authentic Christian spirituality involves a whole way of life. It gives active witness to the dynamic Spirit that motivates and inspires, and it is in harmony with the goals of the people of God and body of Christ. To be a spiritual human being is to admit that there is more to existence than what is encountered through the senses. It is to trust and pray that God is present through the gift grace. It is to be constantly open to God in order to understand who we are and what he asks of his people. Some signs of living spirituality in the Christian community are liturgical renewal, commitment to liberation and social justice issues, renewed honor given to scripture, ecumenical developments, and increased desire for personal experiences of the Spirit. (See also Grace, Morality, Virtue.)

HOLY DAYS   called "holy days of obligation," are special feast days on the church's liturgical calendar. On these days, Catholics who have reached seven years of age are expected to attend Mass and to avoid all unnecessary work.

Six holy days are celebrated by the American Catholic Church. They are: the Solemnity of Mary, Mother of God (January 1st), the Ascension of the Lord Jesus (40 days after Easter Sunday), the Assumption of the Blessed Virgin Mary (August 15th), All Saints' Day (November 1st), the Immaculate Conception of Mary (December 8th), and Christmas Day (December 25th).

These feasts were established at the 3rd Plenary Council of Baltimore during the 19th century.

Four other holy days are celebrated in certain parts of the world but not in the United States. These include: Epiphany (traditionally January 6th), Saint Joseph's Day (March 19th), Corpus Christi (a moveable feast), and the feast day of Saints Peter and Paul (June 29th). (See also Church, Laws of; Liturgical Year.)

HOLY FAMILY, FEAST OF   is the day on which Catholics honor Jesus, Mary, and Joseph as a family. This feast is celebrated each year on the first Sunday after Christmas Day.

Devotion to the holy family became very popular among church members during the 17th century. In 1921, Pope Benedict XV stated that this feast is the one on which the universal church best honors and remembers the holy family. Earlier, Pope Leo XIII had blessed and dedicated all Christian families to the holy family.

The Catholic Church teaches that members of Catholic families ought to look to the life shared by Jesus, Mary, and Joseph as a perfect example of the virtue-filled, pious, and holy lifestyle that every family should lead. (See also Family Ministry, Joseph [Husband of Mary], Mary.)

HOLY WATER   is a sacramental of the church, often used by Catholics as they enter and leave church buildings. At these times they dip the fingers of the right hand into a font or bowl that contains holy water and make the Sign of the Cross.

Holy water is ordinary water that has been blessed by a priest. During this blessing, a special prayer is said that expresses the hope that all who use the holy water will remain free from sinfulness and evil.

Holy water reminds Catholics of the waters of baptism. The use of holy water should also encourage faithful Christians to lead holy lives dedicated to God. Sometimes holy water is used during church ceremonies, for example in the blessing of the congregation at Easter Sunday Mass. Some Catholics continue the practice of obtaining holy water at their parish churches to use in their homes during prayer times. (See also Baptism, Sacramentals, Vestibule.)

HOLY WEEK   is the week during Lent before Easter Sunday. It begins with Palm Sunday and is considered the most holy of weeks during the entire church year.

Holy Week was officially called Passion Week for many years since Christians ponder the death and resurrection of Jesus Christ during this time. Early mention of this holy time is found in the writings of Saint Athanasius. By the 3rd century, holy week began on Good Friday and was concluded with Easter celebrations. By the 6th century Holy Thursday had been added and holy week had been stretched to the full week. In 1955 Pope Pius XII noted that all Catholics should honor Holy Week because of its importance to the church.

On Palm Sunday Catholics receive pieces of blessed palm branches and recall Jesus' entry into the city of Jerusalem. Holy Thursday celebrates the Last Supper of Jesus with his apostles, and centers on his gift of the eucharist. On Good Friday Catholics are invited to think about the death of Jesus during bible readings and a litany of special prayers. Veneration of the cross is an important aspect of Good Friday services. From mid-afternoon Friday until the end of the Easter Vigil Catholics believe that Jesus' body was in the tomb.

On Holy Saturday night the Paschal Candle is lit, baptismal promises are renewed, and converts are often baptized and confirmed. This night is known as the Easter Vigil. Holy Thursday is the day on which the Catholic priesthood was instituted. Catholics are encouraged to pray with other Christians at ecumenical prayer services on Good Friday. (See also Easter, Lent, Liturgical Year.)

HOMILY   is a talk or sermon delivered during the course of a liturgical celebration. The word homily is derived from a Greek term, which means being together. Homilies are often commentaries on the Scriptural readings that help people apply scripture to their daily lives. During Mass the homily follows the gospel reading.

From the writings of Saint Justin we know that homilies were given during the earliest eucharistic celebrations. These talks were delivered most often in a friendly, warm, conversational tone and style. During the Middle Ages, and in later centuries however, homilies became speeches that were quite frequently not related to the themes of liturgical celebrations. The Council of Trent (1545-1563) taught that priests must give sermons related to the scripture texts read at Mass. The real meaning of the homily as a familiar discourse and sharing did not really catch on again until the 20th century.

Vatican Council II taught that homilies should be given during Masses on Sundays, holydays, on the feast days of saints, and on other important church feasts. The council noted that ideally every Mass should have some kind of homily presentation.

The church now stresses that homilies are meant to instruct Catholics about God's Word but should also be given in order to encourage listeners to be more committed to the good news of Christ. At Mass the homily is a link between the Liturgy of the Word and Liturgy of the Eucharist. Brief homilies should be included in communal celebrations of the sacraments of baptism, reconciliation, anointing, and matrimony whenever possible. (See also Bible, Evangelization, Liturgy of the Word/Eucharist.)

HOPE   is one of the three theological virtues (the others are faith and charity). Christian hope is a gift from God given to persons, along with faith and charity, at the time of baptism. It centers on trust and confidence that God offers eternal salvation to all. Hope is a joyful expectation of perfect happiness with God forever.

Saint Paul wrote about hope in his epistles, particularly in his epistle to the Romans and in his letters to the Corinthians. Hope has often been described as a good habit by which an individual trusts that God will grant life everlasting and the means necessary to attain it. This view of hope centers on the individual alone who seeks freedom from sin and life in heaven. While Catholics should yearn for life eternal with God, they should also hope and pray for the liberation of all of humanity from sinfulness, for the continuing perfection of God's kingdom on earth, and for the second coming of Jesus in the Parousia.

The loss or lack of hope is called despair. Despair is experienced when people do not accept that God loves all persons continually, that he never abandons them, and that he remains merciful and forgiving. Some church teachers emphasize that the gift of hope is especially needed by Christians today because of the anxiety, insecurity, discouragement, and frustration of modern life.

While all believers do look to final union and eternal happiness with God, the church teaches that Catholics still ought to work hard to solve the many problems which trouble humanity here and now on earth. Because Jesus has risen from death, believers may face death with great hope, courage, and expect the great joy of heaven. Catholics are urged to pray for hope and confidence in God's promise of salvation, especially when tempted to sin or when suffering physical and mental pains. (See also Heaven, Salvation, Virtue.)

HUMILITY   is a moral virtue that helps people to be honest about their abilities and achievements, and to avoid self-centered pride. Christian humility leads persons to recognize that they are always dependent upon God and that they should praise him for the good that they do. The word humility means humbleness or lowness.

The church holds that selfish pride is the opposite of sincere humility. Persons who are humble thank God for the unique gifts and talents he has given them and for the opportunities to use these gifts to assist others. Persons who are proud often fail to be thankful for their gifts and desire to be independent of their creator and others.

Christian humility is a sincere imitation of Jesus Christ who was always humble, and who sought no empty honors from others. He wanted only to do God's will and to please him. Many of the saints were very humble persons who are good role models for all those who wish to be truly humble Christians.

In 1979 John Paul II described humility as "submission to the power of truth and love." He added that humility is a "rejection of appearance and superficiality" in this life. (See also Fruits of the Spirit, Virtue.)

IMMACULATE CONCEPTION   is a dogma of the Catholic Church that Mary the Mother of Jesus was conceived without original sin. The feast of the Immaculate Conception is celebrated on December 8th as a great solemnity and holy day of obligation.

Pius IX defined the dogma of the Immaculate Conception on December 8, 1854. This teaching was stated *ex cathedra* by the Pope. A church celebration recalling and honoring this long-standing belief had been part of the church's liturgical life for at least 900 years. In 1846 Mary as the Immaculate Conception had been named the patroness of the United States.

The bible does not specifically refer to the Immaculate conception but this teaching is part of the church's sacred tradition. There was much debate about the Church's teachings on the Immaculate Conception during the Middle Ages. The Eastern Catholic Church does not hold this dogmatic teaching about Mary.

The church maintains that Jesus and Mary were the only two persons ever conceived without Original Sin. Official church teachings on the Immaculate Conception are based upon the papal document *Ineffabilis Deus*. Catholics hold that Mary was full of grace at the time of her conception. The church recognizes that there is no way to scientifically prove this, and so it must be held in faith. The Immaculate Conception was a special blessing given to Mary by God since she was to be the mother of Jesus. (See also Holy Days, Mary.)

INDULGENCES   either partial or total, remit temporal punishment due for sins already forgiven. The church is able to grant indulgences to Catholics because of the merits gained by Jesus Christ, and through the spiritual bounty of the entire communion of saints.

The practice of granting indulgences (though stretching back to the early church, at least in principle), got a big boost in the 11th century from Pope Urban II during the Crusades. By the 13th century the church formally accepted that indulgences could be gained through the merits mentioned above. Clement VI inserted this matter in the church's law in 1343. In 1476 Sixtus IV declared that the merits gained by individuals can assist those already in purgatory. Indulgences were granted and dispensed from a *thesaurus*—a church treasury of merits. The practice of granting indulgences was often abused (Martin Luther bitterly complained about Catholics who sold indulgences). The Council of Trent decided that church doctrine on indulgences was legitimate, though Council Fathers regretted the abuses. In 1950 an official church listing of possible indulgences was published.

The doctrine on indulgences, based upon the image of church as Christ's mystical body, has received new emphasis since 1950 when a new theory on indulgences was published in Europe. This theory stressed that the whole church prayerfully intervenes on behalf of the repentant sinner who seeks an indulgence. The legalistic doling-out of indulgences and the indexes (7 years and 500 days, for example) are no longer emphasized. The emphasis is placed upon the goodness of voluntary works of charity and prayerful penance done by Catholics in faith and love.

The church continues to recognize two kinds of indulgences: partial (part of temporal punishment is remitted), and plenary (all of the temporal punishment is wiped away). Indulgences are gained through good works and prayer, and can also be gained for those in Purgatory. In 1967 Paul VI issued *The Doctrine and Practice of Indulgences*. This upholds the teaching about the communion of saints, that each indulgence gained is matched by another one offered through the entire church's spiritual intervention. In 1968 a *Handbook of Indulgences* was published by the church; it places great value on the personal and voluntary works of charity and prayer completed by the faithful. (See also Actual Sin, Charity, Prayer.)

INFALLIBILITY   is a charism or gift given to the church by the Holy Spirit, to protect it from error on matters of faith and the moral life of Christians. It may also be defined as a dogma of the church which states that 1) the pope speaking *ex cathedra* (using his full authority as St Peter's successor), or 2) the Catholic bishops as a body, in union with the pope (as in an ecumenical council) may teach infallibly—without erring—on matters of faith and morality. The term infallibility has Latin roots and means "not able to deceive."

Catholic teaching is that Jesus willed (intended) the church to have infallibility, that he sent the Spirit to guide the community in truth and to help believers speak as genuine witnesses for him (Jn 16:13; Lk 10:16). By the end of the 2nd century, church members relied upon communities founded by the 12 apostles and their close followers to hand down the truths of the faith to converts to the faith. In the 4th century and beyond, special reverence was given to the church of Rome, "St. Peter's community," the center of Christianity and preserver of truth. This reverence carried through the Middles Ages and longer, despite many challenges to the primacy of the Bishop of Rome (the pope) from Eastern-world Christians and Protestant reformers.

Catholics began to accept that the pope had the final word on matters of faith and morals. The great theologian Thomas Aquinas even urged believers to adhere to the pope's decisions because "he cannot err." (The term infallibility was coined by Guido Terreni in the 1300s.) On July 18, 1870 Vatican Council I declared that infallibility was a dogma, that whatever the pope teaches *ex cathedra* must be held by the universal church. In 1964 Vatican II reaffirmed this but made it very clear that the bishops and pope, in unity, can also define teachings in an infallible way.

Papal infallibility has often been interpreted to mean that the pope is incapable of error, that everything he says is immune from error. In fact, the pope (and whole college of bishops with the pope) speaks infallibly only on matters of faith and morals, only when the pope teaches *ex cathedra*, and only when it is explicit that the teaching is binding on the universal church as an absolute decision. Such teachings are called, by some thinkers, irreformable—the way of expressing the great truths (the formulas) may be subject to revision and some discussion, but the essence of the truth cannot be changed.

In ecumenical dialogue the "indefectibility" of the church is discussed. This means that the Spirit guides the church at all times and will not let it go astray from basic gospel truth or the essential life of faith.

Vatican II stated that the pope teaches important truths not as a private person but as supreme teacher and defender of the world-wide church, and that the charism of infallibility is present in him in a unique way. The council also explained how infallible truths may sometimes be expressed by the college of church bishops. Papal infallibility has been formally exercised only twice in recent years: about the Immaculate Conception (by Pius IX in 1854) and about Mary's Assumption (defined by Pius XII in 1950). (See also Dogma, Magisterium, Vatican Council I.)

INSPIRATION   is the method or process by which the Spirit of God guided human beings in the actual composition of biblical writings. The church maintains that the sacred and canonical books of the bible have God as divine author/inspirer, in that he influenced and guided human writers in order that his own divine messages would be communicated.

The church's belief in biblical inspiration springs from the Old Testament belief that Yahweh communicated with the human race directly through such persons as Abraham, Moses, the prophets of Israel, and others. The Israelite people believed that the sacred writings in the Hebrew Scriptures were divinely inspired—especially the five volumes of the Pentateuch (the first five books of the bible). The great Fathers of the Church (during the early centuries of Christianity) held that the bible has its origin and authority in the holy inspiration of God's Spirit. In the Middle Ages the notion that God dictated scripture grew in acceptance and popularity. A great debate among Christian thinkers about how God inspired the human writers arose in the 19th century. Vatican Council I (1870) declared that the church accepts biblical books as sacred since God is their true author through the inspiration of his Spirit. In 1893 Pope Leo XIII stated, in the encyclical *Providentissimus Deus*, that God "incited (human writers) to write, and assisted them in writing so that they correctly conceived, accurately wrote down, and truthfully expressed all that God intended and only what he intended."

The bible is often called the Word Of God. It was written down by human beings who were free to communicate using their own natural powers. They used different literary forms and utilized figures of speech, history, symbols, metaphors, and allusions. Sacred scripture is essential to the preaching, teachings, and ongoing tradition of the Catholic community and is essential to other Christian denominations. The inspired word firmly, faithfully, and without error teaches God's revelation for the sake of humankind's salvation. Through the assistance of biblical *exegesis* (explanation) by theologians and teachers, the church is responsible for interpreting and proclaiming the lasting sacred truth in the bible. God chose human persons and "made use of their powers and abilities, so that with him acting in them and through them, they, as true authors, consigned to writing everything and only those things which he (God) wanted" (See Vatican II's *Dogmatic Constitution On Divine Revelation*, n. 11).

Notes of Interest: The biblical research, analysis, and commentary called *exegesis* is the scientific study of the bible's texts. Exegetes must search out the real intentions and meaning(s) of the writers. Biblical *exegetes* must try to comprehend the religious and cultural factors that influenced the sacred writers. They attempt to help the entire people of God appreciate the content and unity of biblical teaching and God's revelation.

The word *inerrancy* means the inability of the bible to be in fundamental error since God is its supernatural inspirer and divine author. This does not mean that the human writers involved in composing scripture were without error themselves or incapable of making mistakes. Yet it does imply that even though they were capable of committing errors or of including merely personal opinions in their written work, the human writers' limitations do not affect the essential truth of God's revelation. (See also Bible, Books of; Revelation.)

ISAAC   is one of Israel's three great patriarchs; Abraham and Jacob are the other two. Isaac was the son of Abraham and his wife Sarah. His name means "our God smiles" (Gn 21-28).

God made a covenant with Abraham through which he promised that Sarah would have a son, that Abraham would have many descendants, and that he would have a beautiful land where they all could live. Abraham had a son with a slave girl named Hagar. This son, named Ishmael, was not the child promised in the covenant, and he was eventually rejected by Abraham. In her later years Sarah did give birth to Isaac and the covenant between God and Abraham was renewed.

The most famous story about Isaac centers on a command from God to Abraham that he sacrifice his son by killing him. Abraham started to do so but a messenger from God stopped him before he killed Isaac. Many teachers use this story to illustrate how believers should be faithful to God and do what he asks of us, even if his demands are harsh. The story of the sacrifice of Isaac may have been written to teach that human sacrifice is an evil thing.

Paul wrote that Christians should look upon Isaac as a "bearer" of the covenant made by God and Abraham. Isaac was a man who accepted and believed in God. Those who reject God, who are not faithful sons of the Father, are likened to Ishmael, the son who was rejected. (See also Abraham, Jacob.)

ISAIAH   was one of the greatest Israelite prophets. His name means "Yahweh is salvation." Isaiah was born in Jerusalem about 760 B.C., and served as a prophet from 742 to 701. He spoke to God's people about the evils of immorality and sin. He also announced that there were enemies who wanted to attack and conquer the Israelites. The book of Isaiah is the longest book of prophecy in the Old Testament. It is a collection of sayings and poems by Isaiah himself plus writings from a number of his most dedicated followers.

The prophet Isaiah told of Israel's coming destruction yet also foresaw that a remnant of people faithful to God would rise to restore the nation. Isaiah was a well educated, intelligent family man. He lived at the same time as the Hebrew prophets Amos and Hosea.

The first part of Isaiah is probably based on the prophet's actual statements, for example the prophecies about Immanuel and the virgin birth of the promised messiah (see 6-12, 7:14). Another author-poet probably penned chapters 40-55. This section of the book is often referred to as Deutero-Isaiah. Chapters 56-66 were probably composed by a group of Isaiah's followers now sometimes called *the school of Isaiah.*

The prophet is most honored because he called for true reform. He is also remembered for his message about the faithful few, the remnant who would remain Yahweh's chosen nation. Because this book was written by several authors over a rather long period of time, it is sometimes called a "collection of collections" of Isaiah's prophecies. One of Isaiah's most famous statements concerns the king of Israel who would descend from David's family; this prophecy about a royal messiah (11:1-9) is read at the Masses of Christmas Day. (See also Bible, Books of; Old Testament; Prophet.)

JACOB   was the son of Isaac and twin brother of Esau. He lived around 1700 B.C.. His name derives from a Hebrew term that means "God protects." Jacob is one of the three great patriarchs or fathers of the Hebrew people. The 12 tribes of Israel were named after his 12 sons (Gn 25-37 and 42-46).

The book of Genesis says that Yahweh (God) promised Jacob he would have many descendants who would live in a promised land. Jacob worked hard for seven years (a term set by his future father-in-law) to marry a woman named Rachel. He was tricked by his father-in-law and forced to marry Rachel's sister Leah. Seven years later Jacob was able to marry Rachel. She gave birth to Benjamin and Joseph, two of his 12 sons.

The "Jacob stories" in Genesis are well-crafted tales probably not meant to be biographical. Two stories in particular: Jacob stealing the birthright from his brother Esau, and Jacob wrestling with an angel, indicate that God wanted his descendants to gain the promised land.

Jacob inherited the promises that God had made to Abraham, the first patriarch. Even though the Jacob stories are not biographical they do teach about God's care for the salvation of his people. (See also Isaac, Joseph [Son of Jacob], Rachel.)

JEREMIAH was one of the major Old Testament prophets. He preached to the people who lived in the southern part of the kingdom of Judah. Jeremiah foresaw the destruction of Jerusalem, including its great temple, yet his warnings were largely ignored. He also promised the people that Yahweh (God) would one day renew his covenant with the chosen people by writing it on their hearts. The Book of Jeremiah is one of the longest books of the bible.

Jeremiah was born in the town of Anathoth near the city of Jerusalem in the 7th century B.C. He was called by God to be a prophet while still a very young man (626 B.C.), and he delivered stern messages about the tragedies to befall the nation of Israel. The people disliked him because of his prophecies, and he was often the victim of persecution and misunderstanding, even from those he had tried to help. The king and the people refused to listen to Jeremiah's warnings, and so the city of Jerusalem was overrun by foreign armies. Rather than leave the country, Jeremiah decided to remain with the Israelites throughout this period. He died in 587 in Egypt.

The book of Jeremiah is a well-written work that blends history, biography, and prophecy to describe serious problems faced by the Hebrew people. Jeremiah endured great suffering in order to follow his special calling. He often chose to "act out" his more important prophetic statements. For example, he once wore a yoke to symbolize forthcoming suffering and exile.

Jeremiah's prophecies were meant to teach God's chosen nation that their covenant would only be fulfilled if they remained faithful to Yahweh. Jeremiah answered God's difficult call to love and guide the Israelite nation, and he had the courage to speak honestly and forthrightly with and about God. (See also Bible, Books of; Covenant; Prophet.)

JESUS, TITLES OF are some of the various names that have been used over the centuries to describe him. Each title provides a unique perspective on Jesus and tells us something about him. Here are some titles of Jesus.

Jesus Christ, to be completely accurate should be "Jesus, the Christ" (Jesus, the messiah). Though it has become fairly common to hear Jesus of Nazareth called Jesus Christ, Christ is not actually his last name. *Jesus,* from the Hebrew *Yeshua,* means "Yahweh is salvation." This was a common name during Jesus' time. *The Christ,* from the greek *christos,* means "the anointed one." Jesus was called the Christ because his followers believed that he was indeed the true messiah long-awaited by God's chosen people.

Savior is an English word derived from the Latin form of "Jesus." It expresses that God's plan of salvation is brought to fulfillment through Jesus.

Lord is the way Christians referred to Jesus after the Easter-Pentecost event. The word comes from the Greek *kyrios,* which was used of Jesus to express the absolute majesty he has as God, equal to the Father. See the early Christian hymn in Phil 2:1-11, especially the last line.

Son of God is a post-resurrection title that acknowledges Jesus as the one, eternal, only-begotten son of the Father, true God and true man. All persons are sons and daughters of God, but by using the term Son of God, Christians identify Jesus as the divine and human son who is the reflection of God's glory and through whom the Father has spoken. (See Jn 1:1, Rom 9:5, Heb 1:1-4.)

Son of Man is a messianic title that appears over 70 times in the gospels. Jesus used it in speaking of himself (See Lk 9:20-22, Mk 10:33.)

Lamb of God is the title used of Jesus in John's Gospel (1:29). Jesus' disciples recognized the sacrificial nature of his life and death and because the lamb was an important symbol of sacrifice during Old Testament times, Jesus is referred to as the Lamb of God. Through his sacrifice the powers of evil would be abolished in the world.

New Adam indicates that Jesus is the first member, the head, of a whole new generation. He is also "the firstborn of all creatures" who has responded in a perfect way to God's loving revelation. Through the old Adam sin entered human experience; in the New Adam, salvation is possible for all persons (See Col 1:15.)

New Moses reveals what Jesus has accomplished. Through Moses, the great Hebrew leader, the old law and the old covenant were established. Through Jesus, a new law, a new covenant, and a new people of God are established (see Heb 3:1-6 and 8:7-13.)

Mediator is a title of Jesus, who stands between God and humankind and has preserved humanity from estrangement from God. As a perfect go-between he has brought reconciliation and peace to the relationship between people and their God (see 1 Tim 2:5).

Emmanuel is a prophetic name applied to Jesus, which means God-with-us. (See Is 7:14 and Mt 1:22.)

Servant was applied to Jesus, a humble person who sought to serve others lovingly rather than be served himself. He was God's son but he "emptied himself" to become human. Post-resurrection followers of Jesus viewed him as a servant of God who humbly accepted death on a cross for the sake of others (Phil 2:7-8.) He was the suffering servant who has been exalted and glorified by the Father.

Word indicates that Jesus, "spoken by the Father," is the most perfect and definitive revelation (self-communication) of the divine. Jesus is God's own personal, loving word to human beings. The Word is the eternal *logos* who became flesh (See Jn 1:1-18.)

Rabbi is a Hebrew term that means "teacher." Jesus was given this title because he was a wise and knowledgeable man; people were willing to be taught by him (See Jn 20:16; Mk 9:38, 10:20.)

Good Shepherd comes from the Old Testament, in which Yahweh is compared to a shepherd who shows great care and concern for his "sheep," the people Israel (Jer 23 and Ez 34:11-16). In the New Testament Jesus speaks of himself as a good shepherd who guides his flock and even lays down his life for his sheep (See Jn 10:1-18.)

High Priest is how the epistle to the Hebrews depicts Jesus, glorified in the heavenly state, as the high priest over all of creation. (See Heb 4:14-5:10; 8:1-6.)

JOHN   the son of Zebedee was one of the 12 apostles of Jesus. Along with his brother James, he was called to leave his job as a fisherman to follow Jesus. It has been traditionally believed that John is the author of the fourth gospel and of three brief epistles in the New Testament. However, very likely neither the gospel of John nor the Johannine epistles were directly written by John. The gospel was probably composed by a disciple, close to the historical John. It was further refined by another person who was an editor/author. Many agree that the gospel was produced in Asia Minor about 90-100. (Note that the Christian tradition, which claims that John himself wrote the gospel, goes back to Saint Irenaeus and even further back to Polycarp, who may have met John before his death.) Bible scholars hold that the original writer of the gospel of John also composed the first epistle of John (1 John). Some other person, an elder in the very early church community, probably wrote the second and third letters of John.

The Gospel of John was written to show that Jesus revealed

himself as the messiah, Israel's expected-one, and the divine Son of God. It evolved from a very old background of preaching and teaching quite different from the tradition-background of the synoptic versions of the gospel. This explains how some events of Jesus' ministry were to be reported in John but were missing from the synoptic gospels of Mark, Matthew, and Luke.

The gospel of John has a very refined, well thought-out theology. It is referred to as the most theological of the gospels. John describes how the divine Christ shared his light and life, and how he invited people to respond to him in faith. Some of his hearers chose to believe; some could not and these rejected the light and life of Christ. According to church tradition, John did not die a martyr as did the other apostles of Jesus. Saint John's feast day is December 27th. (See also Apostles, Epistles, Gospel.)

JOHN XXIII   is the pope who succeeded Pius XII and was followed by Paul VI. He was born in Italy in 1881. His given name was Angelo Roncalli. He became pope and bishop of Rome in 1958. He is best remembered as the Catholic pontiff who convened the Second Vatican Council (Vatican II). But he is also remembered as a humble, joyous and charming leader.

Angelo Roncalli became a priest in 1904. He was a teacher for many years but he served as a chaplain during World War I. In 1925 he was appointed archbishop and became a diplomat for the Vatican. Thereafter he served in a number of church offices. In 1953 Archbishop Roncalli was named head of the church of Venice as a cardinal. He held this position until he was elected pope. He died of cancer in 1963.

John XXIII was a very forward-thinking pope. He began a complete restudy of the church's code of canon law in 1963. He called for dialogue with other Christian religions, and the World Council of Churches, in order to further the cause of ecumenism. He canonized ten new saints, and he created 52 new cardinals. In 1963 he convened Vatican Council II.

John XXIII was a leader who greatly influenced church life and basic Christian attitudes. Vatican II started a full renewal of Catholicism, a strong movement to reform the church, and studied ways to develop Christian unity. Two of his encyclicals (he wrote eight) have had powerful effects on church life. *Mater et Magistra* emphasized the need for social action, and *Pacem In Terris* was an urgent call for peace among the nations of the earth. John's holiness was officially recognized by Pope Paul VI in 1965 when he began canonization procedures. (See also Paul VI, Pope, Vatican Council II.)

JOHN PAUL I was elected Pope on August 26, 1978. He died a little more than a month later on September 28.

His given name was Albino Luciani. He was born in Italy in 1912 of very poor parents. He was ordained in 1937 and subsequently taught theology, sacred art, and canon law. In December 1958 he was appointed bishop of the diocese of Vittorio-Veneto in Italy. He was created a cardinal by Paul VI on March 5, 1973.

John was an active participant at the meetings of Vatican Council II, and he wrote about his experiences in *Notes on the Council*. He was elected pope, taking the name "John Paul I," on the fourth vote of the conclave—his election was one of the quickest in all of church history. John Paul I is referred to as the "smiling Pope." He was a good man, joyful, warm, and a great witness to Christian living.

Some of John Paul's goals were to lead the church in its efforts to evangelize all of humanity, to promote the ecumenical movement, to work for world peace, and to help the church follow the vision and goals of Vatican Council II. He chose the name John Paul to show that he expected to follow the good example of the two popes who preceded him, John XXIII and Paul VI. His papacy has been called the "September Papacy.' (See also Paul VI, Pope.)

JOHN PAUL II was elected pope on October 16, 1978, after the death of Pope John Paul I. He is the first non-Italian pope since Adrian VI (1522).

John Paul II was born on May 18, 1920 in Wadowice, Poland. His given name is Karol Wojtyla. A hard worker in high school and college, he decided to begin studies for the priesthood in 1942. After his ordination he received a doctorate in theology and taught courses in morality and ethics; he has written many essays and articles for publication. Pius XII named him a bishop in 1958. He later became archbishop—and then cardinal—of the Krakow Archdiocese in Poland.

Archbishop Wojtyla helped represent Polish Catholics at Vatican Council II. He often spoke in favor of basic human rights. As Pope he has supported Vatican II's statements on the dignity of every human person. He has challenged church members to unite as a true community of faithful Christians.

John Paul II—like Paul VI and John Paul I before him—teaches that evangelization is the special duty of the modern church. He has urged the bishops and cardinals to work together in a true spirit of collegiality. During his many trips around the world—to Mexico, Poland, Ireland, the United States, Africa, and elsewhere—he has shown great personal strength, warmth, and humor. His teachings as leader of the church are firm, full of courage, and born of deep conviction and commitment to Catholic faith and Tradtition. (See also John Paul I, Pope.)

JOSEPH (HUSBAND OF MARY)   was the foster father of Jesus and is mentioned in the New Testament and in the gospels of Matthew and Luke. Joseph is a shortened form of the Hebrew name *Jehoseph*, which means "may Yahweh give an increase." Church tradition holds that Joseph was a descendant of King David.

After Joseph and Mary were married, he learned that she was to give birth to a child that was not his. Joseph wanted to hide Mary away to protect her from public shame, but a divine message from God urged him not to do so. It is a tradition of the church that Joseph was present at the birth of Jesus. He died sometime before Jesus began his public ministry. In 1870 Pope Pius IX named Saint Joseph the patron or protector of the Catholic Church and all workers. In 1955 Pius XII announced that the feast of Saint Joseph the Worker would be celebrated on May 1st.

Joseph has often been referred to as a carpenter though he may actually have been a handyman who did various kinds of jobs. Traditionally he has been described as an old man but recent studies indicate that Jewish males commonly married before or quite near their 20th birthdays. For five centuries the feastday of Saint Joseph has been on March 19th. (See also David, King; Holy Family; Mary.)

JOSEPH (SON OF JACOB)   was one of the fathers of the Hebrew people. He was the firstborn of Jacob and Rachel, and the eleventh of Jacob's 12 sons. The story of Joseph is in the book of Genesis, Chapters 37–50.

Joseph was sold into slavery by his brothers who envied his position of favor with Jacob. He was taken by slave traders to Egypt. Because of his prophetic dreams he was named a special aide to the Egyptian pharaoh. He helped the pharaoh by predicting a severe famine. This allowed Egypt to prepare for the famine well in advance. Joseph's brothers, suffering from the famine, came to Egypt to buy grain. Joseph recognized them and forgave them. Eventually they moved to Egypt where they remained for several generations.

Joseph's story is an attempt to relate how Yahweh's chosen people first came to live in the land of Egypt. Joseph died at the age of 110.

Joseph's willingness to help others, his kindness and generosity to people in need, and his ability to forgive his brothers who had wronged him are all qualities that Christians can respect and imitate. (See also Jacob, Moses, Rachel.)

KINGDOM OF GOD   is God's rule or reign over all humanity and the universe. It is also the present church on earth—the kingdom at hand—which is the visible sign of the presence of God's Spirit.

During Old Testament times the Hebrews looked forward to a powerful kingdom of God that would be led by a messiah. During his public ministry Jesus taught that the kingdom was already among and within all persons who repented, believed in God, and loved him and others. This mystery was made clear to his closest followers—the apostles and disciples—after Jesus was raised from the dead and sent the Holy Spirit at Pentecost. Through baptism, by loving God and others, and by holding fast to the church's teachings, every person can belong to the kingdom of God on earth.

The word kingdom is important in Catholic terminology. The church is called the new kingdom, a new Israel and the new people of God. The church is supposed to be a sign of God's concern for humankind and a just society that works toward a perfect kingdom at the end of time. This kingdom should be thought of as God's continuing, active presence among his people, rather than as a particular place.

The church teaches that the idea of the "kingdom already at hand" held a central place in the proclamations of Jesus. His many miracles prove that the kingdom is indeed among us. Vatican Council II taught that the church must remain a visible sign and community whose members become more and more perfect until the end of the world when the true kingdom of God will be fully realized. (See also Ecclesiology, Messiah, People of God.)

LAITY   are full members of the people of God, the church community, who are not ordained ministers or members of religious orders. Vatican Council II emphasized that laypersons are "called to the fullness of the Christian life and to the perfection of charity," and therefore share directly in the priestly, prophetic, and kingly mission of the church. The lay apostolate is participation in the saving mission of the people of God.

By virtue of their baptism laypersons have the duty and mission to spread the good news of Christ, help perfect the secular order, and foster the building of the kingdom in the world to the best of their abilities. There are no second class citizens in the church. Laity, religious, and clergy alike should be treated with respect and dignity, for each have important roles and particular duties in the church's work. Vatican II—in its *Decree on the Apostolate of the Laity*—encourages laypersons to use their unique gifts in evangelizing and serving humanity.

Laypersons are actively involved with the church in many ways. On the local scene (in parish communities) some are catechists/teachers in CCD programs and schools, some belong to parents organizations, some participate in adult education, bible studies, family life programs, singles and young adult ministries, social activities, and programs for the missions and the needy. Some belong to parish councils or boards; some are members of diocesan pastoral councils and various diocesan committees and organizations. On the national scene, in recent decades, the National Councils of Catholic Men and Catholic Women (NCCM, NCCW) and the more recent National Council of Catholic Laity (1971) have been founded. In 1947, the Catholic Family Movement began and, in 1957, the Cursillo Movement was brought to the United States. Organizations such as the Lay Mission-Helpers Association (1955), the Legion of Mary (1921), and *Opus Dei* (1928), and *Pax Christi* (1948) exist for the vocational and spiritual needs of lay people.

In 1980 Pope John Paul II noted that the laity's vocation is participation in the church's mission in diverse ways. The church views formation and training of the laity as essential for true church renewal to take place. In addition to the types of participation and service in the church mentioned above, many lay people serve as lectors (readers at Mass), as special ministers—or extraordinary ministers—of the eucharist, as music ministers, evangelizers, youth ministers, ministers to the divorced and separated, and in other forms of ministry. (See also Lay Ministries, Parish, People of God.)

LAY MINISTRIES   are forms of Christian service rendered to the church by baptized persons as a response to their call to witness to Christ. Some generally accepted lay ministries are: 1) ministry of hospitality, 2) ministry of the word, 3) ministry of the bread and cup, and 4) ministry of music.

In the early church the apostles and other disciples could not perform all the ministry tasks required by the growing Christian community. Deacons and deaconesses were chosen to help them by caring for the sick, preaching, assisting in baptism and eucharist ceremonies, etc. Other gifted persons were called to ministerial service when particular needs arose within the community. Gradually, over the centuries, lay ministries diminished as more and more such roles were assumed by priests and religious. Since Vatican Council II there has been a renewed sense among Catholics that through baptism all Christians are called to service in the church (1 Cor 12:4-11). In 1972 Paul VI issued an apostolic letter, *Ministeria Quaedam*, which provided for reform of liturgical ministries in the church. This document abolished the minor orders and two liturgical ministries were opened up to the laity: ministry of reader and ministry of acolyte. New rites for the official institution of persons into these ministries have been developed. This document also left open the possibility for additional lay ministries, such as the ministry of catechesis. The individual tasks of the four primary lay ministries are:

Minister of Hospitality, often called an usher, welcomes those who enter the church for worship. He or she sees that worshippers are seated and that the building remains comfortable throughout the celebration. Sometimes this person also assists with the offertory processions, distributes parish bulletins and other materials, and sees that the church building is neat and orderly after every ceremony. These ministers also help to collect money offered in support of the church. Through his or her friendly manner and welcoming attitude, the minister of hospitality sets a positive tone for the liturgy to be celebrated.

Minister of the Word, also called a reader or lector, proclaims the first and/or second reading during Mass, but never the gospel reading, which must be done by the celebrant or deacon. Study, practice, and prayer help persons to be good and effective ministers of the word for the people of God.

Minister of the Bread and Cup, referred to as an extraordinary minister, or a special minister of the eucharist, helps to distribute communion during Mass. He or she might also take the eucharist to the sick, the dying, or to shut-ins who can't get to the church building. Local pastors must petition the bishop before persons can be official ministers of the bread and cup. These persons must then participate in the rite of institution.

Minster of Music assumes one of several possible roles: musician, choir director, song leader, or cantor. Choir members and composers are not usually considered to be music ministers. Since liturgical music enhances the community's expression of faith and reverence, the minister of music helps worshippers to rediscover and deepen faith commitments.

Note of Interest: Laypersons often participate in these particular ministries, as well as men and women who belong to religious orders and men preparing for the *diaconate*. (See also Laity, Ministry, Parish.)

LENT is a period of forty days during the church's liturgical year, which begins on Ash Wednesday and ends on Holy Saturday (the day before Easter). The word Lent comes from the Middle English *lente* and the German *lenz* which means "spring." Lent is time for *metanoia* (conversion or re-conversion to the Christian way),—It is a time for prayer, penance, and works of charity for others. It is also a time for Christians to turn away from sinfulness and evil—to have a change of heart—as they prepare for the joyous feast of Easter.

Traditionally Lent has been a time dedicated to the remembering of the forty days that Jesus spent fasting and and praying in the desert to prepare for his ministry. Before Lent was officially observed for 40 days Christians observed weekly days of fasting and penances, usually the Wednesdays and Fridays of each week.

From the very beginning Lent has been an opportunity for *metanoia* (change of heart), for embracing a lifestyle focused on God's grace and justice and for turning from sinful ways. Lent is a season of repentance and hope for church members. Like Springtime itself, each lenten season can be a time for spiritual rebirth and renewal. Vatican Council II noted that it is appropriate for Christians to read the bible and to participate in scripture-centered prayer services during Lent.

Note of Interest: Present church laws require very little penance compared to past laws. In this country all lenten Fridays are days of abstinence—no meat or meat products may be eaten on these days. Ash Wednesday and Good Friday are days of abstinence plus fasting—only one full meal and two smaller meals may be consumed. Lenten regulations and rules vary from country to country. (See also Conversion, Holy Week, Liturgical Year.)

LITURGICAL YEAR is the cycle of seasons and feasts celebrated by the Catholic Church in the course of a year. This cycle is sometimes referred to as the church year or the liturgical calendar. The cycle begins on the first Sunday of Advent and it includes five major seasons: Advent, Christmas, Lent, Easter, and Ordinary Time.

A universal liturgical calendar of feast days was published by Pope Pius V in 1568. Since then many feasts and celebrations have been added to this calendar. Vatican Council II declared that the total number of feasts on the calendar should be restricted. The bishops observed that the major feasts of the liturgical year can lead to great faith through "pious practices for soul and body," instruction, prayer, works of charity, and penances they offer.

The entire cycle of the liturgical year centers on Jesus Christ's mission and ministry of salvation and, in a special way, his paschal mystery. The liturgical year also offers Catholics a fine opportunity to remember and honor Mary, the mother of Jesus, and the saints.

The liturgical year is not a mere representation of past events but rather a celebration of Christ living in the church. Feast days of saints are observed because they fully entered into the mysteries of Christ's life, death and resurrection. These can be classified as feastdays, solemnities, moveable feasts, and holy days. (Those special feasts called holy days of obligation are listed under Holy Days.) The seasons of the liturgical calendar are as follow:

Advent: 1st Sunday after Nov. 30th—the feast of Saint Andrew—until Dec. 24th.

Christmas: Dec. 25th until the Sunday after Epiphany.

Lent: Ash Wednesday until Holy Saturday—the day before Easter.

Easter: Easter Sunday until Pentecost.

Ordinary Time: between Christmas and Lent; also the weeks after Pentecost until the end of the liturgical year. (See also Christmas, Easter, Holy Days.)

LITURGY OF THE WORD/EUCHARIST   are the two main parts of the eucharistic celebration called the Mass. The Liturgy of the Word centers on the proclamation of God's Word (scripture), while the Liturgy of the Eucharist includes the consecration of bread and wine, the Great Amen, and the sharing of the eucharist by all gathered. These two parts of the Mass were formerly referred to as the Mass of Catechumens and Mass of the Faithful.

During the liturgy of the Word passages from the Bible— usually with a common theme—are read. When there are three readings (as on Sundays, for example), the first is taken from the Old Testament, the second from an epistle, Acts of the Apostles, or the Book of Revelation (the Apocalypse), and the third reading is always a gospel passage. A homily based on the readings follows. Next all pray the Nicene Creed aloud as a profession of faith. This is followed by the Prayers of the Faithful, which are petitions from the assembly for the needs of the church, the salvation of the world, and for the local community.

The Liturgy of the Eucharist includes the preparation of the gifts of bread and wine, the eucharistic prayer, the consecration (Jesus becomes fully present under the forms of simple bread and wine), the Great Amen of the whole assembly, the Lord's Prayer, the sign of peace shared by all, and then the reception of the eucharist in communion in the form of bread, or bread and wine.

The divisions are as follows:

Introductory Rites: Entrance Song or Hymn, Greeting, Penitential Rite, Lord, Have Mercy, Glory to God, Opening Prayer.

Liturgy of the Word: Readings (First Reading, Responsorial Psalm, Second Reading, Verse, Gospel), Homily, Profession of Faith (Creed), Prayer of the Faithful.

Liturgy of the Eucharist: Offertory Song, Preparation of the Gifts (Offertory Procession), Washing of the Hands, Prayer Over the Gifts.

Eucharistic Prayer:
Preface
Thanksgiving
Holy, Holy, Holy Acclamation
Consecration of Bread and Wine
Memorial Acclamation
Doxology and Great Amen.

Communion Rite: Lord's Prayer, Sign of Peace, Lamb of God and Breaking of the Bread, Communion, Communion Song or Hymn, Prayer After Communion.

Concluding Rite: Announcements, Blessing of Assembly, Dismissal. (See also Bible, Eucharist, Worship.)

LUKE is one of the four evangelists of the New Testament. He is Author of the Gospel of Luke and the Acts of the Apostles. The Gospel of Luke is one of the so-called synoptic gospels. Very likely it was written in the city of Rome about 75-78 A.D. Luke was Greek, a gentile or non-Jewish person, who may have been a doctor. He was friend and travelling companion to Saint Paul.

It is traditionally believed that Luke did actually compose the two-volume work of the Gospel of Luke and the Acts of the Apostles. This particular belief dates back to at least the 2nd century. He remained unmarried throughout his life and was in his eighties when he died in the Middle East. In one of his epistles (Col 4:14), Saint Paul refers to Luke as his "dear friend" and as a "doctor."

Luke's gospel reveals that Jesus was truly a person who cared for the poor, the suffering, and the sinners of this world. It was probably written more for Gentile Christians than for Jewish Christians. The Gospel of Mark, written earlier, was one of Luke's most important resources for composing his version of the good news about Jesus.

The Gospel of Luke shows Jesus' true love and compassion for all who are burdened by sin and suffering. It stresses that the good news of salvation was proclaimed for all of humanity. Luke's gospel includes unique introductory information about the birth and childhood of Jesus' life. This information does not appear in the other gospels. Saint Luke's feastday is October 18th. (See also Acts of the Apostles, Gospel, Synoptics.)

MAGISTERIUM is the teaching authority or teaching office of the church. The term can also accurately refer to the body of church leaders/teachers who define official Catholic doctrines. Magisterium derives from the Latin *magister*, which means "teacher." The members of the church's official magisterium proclaim truths about matters of Catholic belief and morality authoritatively and authentically.

The first persons who had this special authority were Saint Peter and the other apostles, who received it from Jesus. Gradually through the early centuries of Christianity, catechists, teachers, deacons, and priests became more and more directly subject to the authority of their bishops. When heresies challenged the church, prior to the Middle Ages, bishops became the authentic authoritative, magisterial teachers in their dioceses. By the 13th century the pope had become the powerful magisterial teacher, often simply expecting Christians to fully accept (without any question) the doctrines he proclaimed. Over the ages two classes developed in the church: those who taught (teachers, priests, and bishops), and the learners (all others). In recent years this separation mentality has changed. Every person is a lifelong learner and every person has something to teach others.

The modern emphasis on collegiality in the church has helped the hierarchy and other members of the people of God to be more open to numerous points of view, and to rely less on strictly authoritative statements about the church. In a broad sense the magisterium can refer to the whole church membership, and not merely to the ordained hierarchy and theologians in good-standing. All baptized persons in the church have a duty to participate in the mission of the community, which definitely includes proclaiming the gospel and the teaching ministry. In certain circumstances, after reflection and prayer, Catholics may have to form and follow their consciences, even if this means dissent from official teachers.

The official teaching authority of the church, the magisterium, can be called the teacher of the truth, according to Vatican II. It is a kind of channel through which the great tradition of Catholics can be known. The church exercises an extraordinary magisterium through the teaching during Ecumenical councils or by the pope alone speaking infallibly (*ex cathedra*). An ordinary magisterium is exercised through papal encyclicals, Vatican decrees, synod teachings, conferences of bishops, and even by individual church leaders teaching the faithful. Catholics are taught to faithfully respect and assent to authentic, magisterial teachings. (See also Collegiality, Doctrine, Infallibility.)

MARK   is the author of the first and the shortest of the four gospels, which was written around 65 A.D. His gospel, second in the New Testament, between the books of Matthew and Luke, is one of the so-called synoptic gospels.

Mark was a Jew from Jerusalem who was sometimes called John Mark. He was a close friend of Saint Peter and he also knew St. Paul. It is very probable—as reported in the Acts of the Apostles—that Mark went along with Paul when he conducted his first missionary trip. Saint Mark later wrote his gospel in Rome. He died a martyr in Alexandria after founding the church in that city.

Mark's Gospel was written for non-Jews who wanted to become Christians. Mark wanted to show how Jesus Christ was indeed the promised messiah, the Son of God, who saves all of humanity from evil and promises eternal salvation. He dwells on the daily actions and details of Jesus' public life to show this. It is sometimes erroneously concluded that the Gospel of Mark is not as refined or theologically sophisticated as the other three gospel versions.

St. Mark was inspired by God to reveal that all persons can enjoy happiness with God forever as a result of the death and resurrection of Jesus Christ. The Church celebrates his feastday on April 25th. (See also Gospel, Inspiration, Synoptics.)

MARY   is the mother of Jesus, the wife of Saint Joseph, and the greatest of all the saints. She is a model of faithful living for all Christians. Mary is often called the Blessed Virgin because she so freely and completely responded to God's Will that she conceived Jesus by the power of the Holy Spirit. She continued to do God's will throughout her life on earth. The church teaches that Mary was conceived without sin and was assumed into heaven with body and soul united. Since 1964 she has been honored as the mother of the church.

It is traditionally believed, though not historically proven, that Mary was the daughter of Joachim and Anne. She conceived Jesus through the power of the Spirit (Lk 1:26–38, Mt 1:18–25), and she married Joseph, an upright Jewish man from Nazareth. Not much else is known about Mary's life. The New Testament mentions her in the infancy narratives and describes how she attended a wedding at Cana with Jesus. She was present at the crucifixion, and she was with Jesus' followers at Pentecost. The church has always given Mary a special place of honor. She has been called the new Eve; the first Eve brought sin and death to the world, but Mary was the bearer of life. At the Council of Ephesus in 431 Mary was named the true mother of God, and a model of Christian living in her total surrender to the Father. Belief in the Assumption was widespread by the 700s, and the church was celebrating the Annunciation, Purification, Assumption, and the birth of Mary by the mid-800s. Celebration of Mary's Immaculate Conception became popular 150 years later. (Saint Bernard of Clairvaux is considered the greatest Mariologist in church history.) In 1950 the Assumption dogma was defined. In 1953 Pius XII declared a Marian Year. The proclamation of the Immaculate Conception dogma took place on December 8, 1854.

Mary had complete trust in God.

Vatican Council II placed its teachings on Mary in the *Dogmatic Constitution on the Church* to highlight Mary's role as mother of the church.

The church believes that Mary is a living symbol of the way in which every person should respond to God's grace with faith, hope, and love. She is given a special place in Christian life because of her unique relationship to Jesus. She has been called the archetype and the prototype of the body of Christ, the church (since the church understands that it is the "bride of Christ" and is symbolized in Mary's marvelous faith). Mary is revered as the mother of Jesus, and as the greatest in the communion of saints who constantly intercedes on behalf of others. She was a human being, not a superhuman goddess, and her faith and holiness make her worthy of imitation by all Christians. The American bishops issued the Marian statement, *Behold Your Mother*, in 1970. (See also Assumption of Mary, Immaculate Conception, Holy Family.)

MATRIMONY   is one of the seven sacraments of the church. Through this sacrament, a man and a woman are united as husband and wife. Married couples are called by the church to be visible signs of the union that exists between Jesus Christ and his church. Certain conditions must be met in order that a marriage be considered valid by the church. The man and woman must be of legal age and neither should have been married previously (unless a church annulment of the previous marriage has been granted); both partners must be able and willing to have sexual intercourse; both must be willing to have children, if possible. The couple may not be blood-relations.

Nuptial Masses for Christian marriages began to be celebrated about the 4th century. By the Middle Ages, the church had declared that a priest should be present at all marriage ceremonies as the official representative of the church. At that time the church also began to stress that marriages were legal contracts rather than covenant relationships. In the 1440s the Council of Florence declared that matrimony should be regarded as one of the church's seven sacraments. The Council of Trent (mid-1500s) reaffirmed that matrimony is a sacrament which, in order to be valid, must take place in the presence of an ordained Catholic priest.

Jesus obviously believed that the bond between married persons could not be abolished. Saint Paul wrote about married life, likening it to the permanent bond that exists between the risen Jesus and the church community (Ephesians, Chapter 5). Current thinking in the church emphasizes that a valid marraige is a permanent union (until the death of one of the partners), between two persons. The man and woman who enter into a covenant through matrimony are the primary ministers of the sacrament. The priest (or deacon), the official witnesses, and the others gathered for the ceremony and celebration affirm that a loving union/covenant has been established.

The sacrament of marriage is intended to help men and women to love faithfully, to grow in holiness, and to raise their children as members of the church. The Christian family is often referred to as "the domestic church." In marriage men and women are equal partners; both are human beings with personal dignity. The church encourages married couples to be loving symbols to each other and to all of humankind of God's continuing love and concern. By being considerate, loving parents, married people cooperate in God's ongoing work of creation in an important way. (See also Divorce, Family Ministry, Sacrament.)

MATTHEW   is one of the twelve apostles of Jesus, and is credited as the "author" of the Gospel of Matthew. Matthew's Gospel is placed at the beginning of the New Testament and was probably composed about 80–85. Matthew is venerated as a saint of the church. His name comes from the Hebrew and means "gift of Yahweh."

Matthew was also called Levi and before being called to follow Jesus he was a tax-collector or publican for the Roman government (Mt 9:9). Not much else is known for certain about his life. It is believed that he was martyred, and a church tradition claims that some relics of his body were discovered in Salerno in 1080. The Gospel of Matthew was written in Aramaic (by a number of authors/editors) for Jewish Christians living in Palestine. Probably, two resources used in the composition of this gospel version were Mark's Gospel and a document known as "Q." The Gospel of Matthew was a favorite among early Christians; it was often used in worship ceremonies and as a basis for preaching.

In the Gospel of Matthew Jesus is depicted as the true messiah, the anointed one (the Lord), long-awaited by Israel, God's people on earth. The gospel has five major sections and contains five important discourses (teachings), including the famous Sermon on the Mount. It is likely that the five sections and five discourses symbolize the New Law offered by Jesus (as compared to the Old Law in the first five books of the Old Testament). Jesus, the messiah and teacher, is the new Moses who begins a new people of God.

Matthew's gospel is sometimes called the gospel of the kingdom (the word kingdom appears in it over 50 times), and it was written to urge belief in Jesus as messiah and savior. Composers of Matthew's gospel were very interested in illustrating how the 12 apostles were called and united as the original Christian community and in how the church, the new kingdom and new people of God was founded. Catholics celebrate Matthew's feast day on September 21st each year. (See also Gospel, Kingdom of God, Synoptics.)

MEDALS   are sacramentals of the church made from metallic substances that usually have a religious picture or words on them. Catholics may wear medals on neck-chains or carry them in purses or pockets.

Medals were used in the early church. Saint Genevieve received one from Saint Germain during the 5th century, for example. Medals to honor the popes were made first in the 15th century and the official blessing of these sacramentals was begun by Pope Pius V in the 1500s. In 1830 the mother of Jesus appeared to Catherine Laboure in France and told her that a Miraculous Medal of the Immaculate Conception should be created and that devotion to Mary should be promoted (though this was a private revelation, many Catholics choose to believe it).

Medals are not to be considered lucky charms or magical items that have special powers. Yet many Catholics believe that medals help those who wear them to grow in faith and hope. A favorite medal is still the scapular—which was promoted by Pius X in 1910. It has a picture of Jesus on one side and an image of Mary on the other side.

Medals may be blessed by priests and some indulgences may be granted to persons who wear or carry certain medals; among these are: 1) the miraculous medal, 2) the medal of the child Jesus, 3) the medal of Our Lady of Guadalupe, 4) the Saint Benedict medal, and 5) the medal of Saint Bernard. (See also Indulgences, Sacramentals.)

MESSIAH   is a Hebrew term which means "the anointed." The comparable Greek word is *christos*, which translates into English as "the Christ." Catholics believe that Jesus Christ is the promised messiah who brings the good news of salvation to all of humanity.

The Israelite people waited many centuries for a messiah who would be a strong military leader, and a kingly ruler who would defeat their foes and restore the kingdom of Israel to power and greatness. It was expected that this leader would be something of a superhuman person. The burning hope for a strong, warlike messiah had begun to wane toward the close of the Old Testament era.

Jesus did not view himself as the powerful, royal messiah-ruler so long awaited by the Jewish people. He was probably more comfortable with the title Son Of Man, which identified him as an important spiritual guide and humble leader, sent by God to care for his people on earth. The early Christians, including the gospel writers (the evangelists), recognized and preached that Jesus was indeed the promised Messiah from God. The synoptic gospels indicate that Jesus did claim to be the promised messiah. The Gospel of John also notes this (Mk 14:61ff, Mt 26:63ff and Jn 10:24). The gospel writers understood that Jesus Christ's true messianic mission was to be a humble, spiritual guide—one who would suffer for his people—rather than to be a powerful, political man and conquerer of Israel's enemies.

Catholics believe that Jesus is the Son of God, the holy person consecrated and anointed by God to save humankind from sin and evil. As the savior and promised messiah he helps the human race attain the eternal happiness of heaven. The name Jesus Christ really means "Jesus, the anointed one" or "Jesus the Messiah." The word *Christ* was not Jesus' personal last name. (See also Anointing; Humility; Jesus, Titles of.)

MINISTRY is any form of active Christian service, designated or commissioned by the church to aid the community in meeting the needs of its members and to help the church to fulfill its mission to proclaim the good news of salvation in Jesus Christ. The mission of the church and its many ministries are not the same thing. Ministries help the church fulfill its mission. Their reason for being and their true source is the universal mission of spreading the gospel. This mission was given to the apostles and thus to the entire body of Christians by Jesus himself (Mt 28:16-20). Persons who become active in ministry within the church are referred to as ministers (as in catechetical ministers, youth ministers, or pastoral ministers). The church has both ordained and non-ordained ministers. Actually all baptized members of the community have a right and responsibility to be ministers to others and should participate in the church's saving mission on a daily basis.

Christian ministry (in all its forms) is an extension of the mission and ministry of Jesus. The earliest chosen followers of Jesus, the apostles, considered themselves persons engaged in ministry (Mk 10:45, Acts 1:17). The New Testament word for such service is the Greek *diakonia*—performing actions that build up the body of Christ, the new people of God. Paul believed that the Spirit gives many gifts (charisms) to individual members of the body to enable them to minister to others in humble, selfless ways (Eph 4:7-11; 1 Cor 12:4-11). From the 2nd century on, the definition of *ministry* narrowed. It included, usually, only ordained men in the church—bishops, priests, deacons. The term gradually acquired connotations of power, influence, and authority in the Catholic Church. Since Vatican Council II (1960s), the original meaning of ministry has been actively reclaimed. More church members, especially laypersons, have begun to participate actively in church ministries.

With increased participation in ministries there has been a corresponding increase in awareness of the true vitality and broad variety of ministries open to the people of God. The Christian community has a distinct, overriding (saving) mission and the church recognizes that many persons receive gifts (or charisms, or grace) from the Spirit to bring this mission to fulfillment. She calls these persons through baptism, confirmation, and orders to exercise their ministries that prepare for God's great kingdom-coming. It is the power of the Spirit, more than the earthly power of the institutional church, that is at work in individual Christians who are called to ministry.

In 1972 Paul VI wrote (in his apostolic letter, *Ministeria Quedam*) that church members should no longer think of certain ministries as mere steps ascending toward the ordained priesthood. He declared that two ministries—those of *reader* and *acolyte*—are now valid lay ministries, and he left open to future decision whether or not there will be other official ministries for laypersons. Vatican II taught that there is a variety of ministries, which work for the good of the whole body and toward a common goal—the salvation of humankind in Jesus through the spread of his good news. In the United States, the *National Catechetical Directory: Sharing the Light of Faith* indicates that the ministries of word, service, and worship bind church members closely, and that all other forms of Christian ministry somehow fall within their scope. (See also Baptism, Orders, People of God.)

MIRACLES   are marvelous events or moments in which God's saving power and holy presence are manifested. It is believed by all Catholics that Jesus had miraculous powers and performed a number of miraculous works such as calming a raging sea, feeding a large group of people (with very little food available), and raising people from the dead. The word miracle derives from the Latin words *miraculum*, "a marvel," and *mirari*, "to wonder."

Many of the church's official statements on miracles come from Vatican Council I (1870). It is said that Jesus' miraculous deeds were signs of God's revelation in him. Vatican II recognized Jesus' miracles in its document on *Divine Revelation*.

Certain marvelous, miraculous events (or signs) did occur during Jesus' ministry, but it is difficult to identify or prove in a scientific way just what happened during these events. Miracles were central to Jesus' ministry/mission and they strengthened the faith of those who were witnesses to them. Some people dismiss the whole notion of biblical miracles (saying they didn't occur), others interpret them fundamentally (saying they happened exactly as recorded in scripture), and still others hold that it's not important if they took place or not (faith in God's saving power and revelation, which miracle stories express, is what really counts).

The church specifies that Jesus worked miracles, that this has been held since the beginning, and that miracles deepen the faith of church members. The gospels indicate that miracles or signs were an essential part of the proclamation of the good news of the kingdom (Mt 11:4–5). Of the many miracles reported, the greatest miraculous event was the resurrection of Jesus by God. (See also Bible, Faith, Revelation.)

MISSIONS are places around the world where the good news of Jesus Christ has not been widely known and/or accepted. The term missions comes from the Latin *missio*, meaning "sending." The universal church has a mission, received from Jesus himself, to spread the gospel message throughout all parts of the world. The church establishes particular missions, at various geographical locations, in order that the good news of salvation can be preached and acts of charity and mercy can be performed. Every member of the church is called, through baptism and commitment to Christ, to do his or her part in fulfilling the overall mission of the church. Certain dedicated enthusiastic individuals are sent in the name of the church community as missionaries to the many missions in the world.

All through its history the church has attempted to preach the gospel and to spread the teachings of Christ. Such missionary activity has often led to great physical suffering and personal sacrifice on the parts of dedicated missionaries (some have been tortured and/or killed). Catholics and other Christians recognize that the apostles were missionaries in a special sense. They were commissioned by the risen Jesus himself to spread the good news to humanity (see Mk 3:13ff.; Mt 28:16–20). Saint Paul was a model of Christian missionary work; his travels and ministry of evangelization are discussed at length in the Acts of the Apostles.

The church is truly "catholic"—a universal community that invites all men and women to join its body. Yet such universal catholicity remains a goal and an ideal. In this age the church still hopes to reach all parts of the world in order to effectively preach the gospel and to spread the spirit of Christianity. Various means by which Catholics participate in the church's work include: service in foreign countries and cultures; service among unchurched peoples and/or non-practicing church members; by evangelizing wherever and whenever the opportunity arises; through financial contributions, gifts of medical supplies, and other donated goods. Prayer and personal sacrifice for the building of the kingdom of God are other acts that can support missionary works.

Vatican Council II issued the *Decree on the Church's Missionary Activity* which clearly expressed the church's belief that it is missionary by nature and that each baptized person has a responsibility to do his or her part in sharing the good news of

Jesus Christ. The council added that church missions, at home and abroad, must center on effective evangelization and the implanting of the church (community) among those peoples and groups where it has not yet taken root. Missionaries have an urgent, special vocation to witness to the gospel.

The church annually observes World Mission Day. On World Mission Day in 1981 Pope John Paul II noted that a church without a missionary commitment is an incomplete church or a sick church. He called upon the people of God to think about the true mission of the entire community and how evangelization is critical to the future of the world. (See also Evangelization, Witness, Works of Mercy.)

MONOTHEISM   is belief in the existence of only one God and the worship of that God. The word comes from two Greek terms, *monos*, which means single, and *theos*, which means god. *Polytheism* is belief in and worship of many different gods. This word comes from the Greek *polus*, meaning many, and *theos*, meaning god.

Judaeo-Christian belief is that there is but one, true God and that this God has freely chosen to reveal himself (make a loving self-communication), to all people. The Hebrews of old had faith in Yahweh, the God of the patriarchs, the one God who revealed himself to Abraham, brought the chosen people out of slavery in Egypt, and made them a great nation. He established a loving friendship-agreement, a covenant-relationship with them. This monotheistic belief of the Israelite people was in stark contrast to the polytheistic beliefs and practices of many of their neighbors, the Babylonians, Egyptians, Phoenicians, and others.

Christian people, including Catholic Christians, are monotheistic. They believe that a new covenant between the one, true God and all of humanity has been established through God's most perfect revelation and word, Jesus Christ. They maintain that God is the only God, and that no other gods should be placed before him. To place another god before the true God is to commit idolatry. Some of the aspects or qualities of the one God are: God has one divine nature, yet is three persons, Father, Son, and Spirit. The one, true God is all-holy, all-loving, all-good, faithful, all-wise, and all-knowing. God is the infinite and the creator, the origin and single source of all that exists. The one God is transcendant, distinct from this world, a wholly other, yet somehow also mysteriously personal and present to and even within people. (See also Trinity, Yahweh.)

MORALITY centers upon the new command that Jesus handed on in the gospels "to love one another as I have loved you." Words and deeds are most truly Christian when they are based on this precept. The term morality derives from the Latin *moralis*, which means "custom."

In Old Testament times the Hebrews adhered to the covenant established between themselves and Yahweh. They were also guided by the Law of Moses (which includes the Ten Commandments (Dt 5:6–21). Jesus Christ did not do away with the old law, rather he fulfilled and perfected it. The morality of Jesus is built upon the two great commandments of the old law: 1) Love God with your whole heart, whole soul, whole mind, and whole strength; and 2) Love your neighbor as yourself (Mk 12:30–31, Lk 10:27, Mt 22:36–40). These commandments were part of the Law of Moses and the moral code of Israel (Dt 6:5, Lv 19:18). Jesus added a new dimension to the requirement of love: Be willing to give your life in love. He calls us to trust in his good news, to turn from sin, and to seek salvation in the kingdom-at-hand. It is interesting that in the gospels there are no moral or ethical codes presented in a systematic way. Over the centuries the church has sifted through Jesus' teachings to determine what is and what is not moral, based on Jesus' new command.

People are called to love God, but love and concern for *others* is also essential. All of our destinies are linked or bound in an intimate way. To be moral persons Christians must seek to do God's will while recognizing their ongoing responsibility to others, particularly the poor, the suffering, and the oppressed.

Some specific guidelines that assist Christians to live morally are the Ten Commandments, the beatitudes, the corporal and spiritual works of mercy, teachings on the virtues, and church precepts.

Note of Interest: There are many issues today that call for Christian responses. Some of the most striking of these are: violation of human rights, abortion, euthanasia, suicide, racism, and prejudice, human sterilization, capital puinishment, and nuclear arms buildup. (See also Charity, Conversion, Free Will.)

MOSES was a great Old Testament leader and one of the founders of the nation of Israel. He led the Hebrews out of slavery in Egypt and helped them to make a covenant with God. The name Moses has Egyptian roots and means "one who is born."

Moses lived about 1200 years before the birth of Jesus Christ and was the son of Hebrew parents. The book of Exodus describes how as a baby he was hidden in a basket by his mother and sister. They placed the basket in the river so that the Egyptians would not find the baby and kill him. Moses was saved by an Egyptian princess, and he grew up in a royal palace. He knew all along that he was a Hebrew, and when he got older he killed an Egyptian to defend the life of a Hebrew man. He fled to the land of Midian where he became a shepherd. One day Moses saw Yahweh (God) in a "burning bush." God told him to return to Egypt to ask the pharaoh to free the Hebrews from slavery. Moses and his brother, Aaron, gave pharaoh God's message, but pharaoh refused to free the Hebrews. God then sent ten plagues to punish Egypt. Eventually with Moses as leader, the Hebrews escaped from Egypt (their escape is called the "exodus"), and they went into the desert in search of the promised land. While in the desert Moses received the Ten Commandments from God on Mount Sinai, and he helped the people seal a covenant with Yahweh.

Few facts about Moses can be historically established, yet he is honored as a great lawgiver who taught God's people about his love and concern for them. Moses is remembered as the leader who united the Hebrews so that they could become the nation of Israel. Vatican Council II pointed out that through Moses God promised to take care of and guide his chosen people as long as they remained faithful to their promise to love him.

Moses was one of God's special servants. He is mentioned more often than any other Old Testament figure by the writers of the New Testament. Moses led the Hebrews from slavery in Egypt, and Jesus Christ, the new Moses, proclaims God's love and saves people from slavery to sin and evil. (See also Covenant, Passover, Pentateuch.)

NEW TESTAMENT   is that portion of the bible that tells about the life, death, and resurrection of Jesus Christ and about the beginnings of the church. It contains the four gospels plus a number of other writings: The Acts of the Apostles, the epistles, and the Book of Revelation (also called the Apocalypse). There are 27 books in the New Testament. Most of the original writing of these books was done in Greek. The english word "Testament" stems from the Latin *testamentum*, which means "covenant" or "agreement."

By the end of the 4th century these 27 books (and only these) were considered part of the New Testament. In the year 405 Pope Innocent I confirmed this. The Council of Trent (16th century), stated authoritatively that the four gospels, the epistles, Acts, and

Revelation complete the New Testament of the bible.

The gospel writers, Matthew, Mark, Luke, and John attempted to show the importance of the life and ministry of the Lord rather than to compose biographies. The epistles, Acts, and Revelation were written to show how the early Christians developed in their understanding of Jesus as God's son and the risen Savior. The New Testament books are listed under Bible, Books of. (See also Bible, Epistle, Gospel.)

NOAH is the biblical hero of the great flood ("the deluge") story in the book of Genesis. He is also known as the original cultivator of vineyards. According to the bible, Noah was the son of Lamech, and was the father of Shem, Ham, and Japheth. Because he was heroic, upright and just during the time before the great deluge, Noah has been called the second father of humankind and the ancestor of the human race following the flood. The name Noah (or Noe) is derived from a Hebrew verb that means "to give rest."

Noah received instructions from God to build an ark so that he and his family, plus one male and one female of every kind of animal would be saved from the coming flood waters. (God had decided to destroy the earth and all its inhabitants because it was filled with evil.) Noah was in the ark during "40 days and 40 nights" of rain, 150 days in all before the water subsided. He survived because he was a righteous man, sinless and full of virtue in God's eyes. After Noah and his family emerged from the ark, the whole earth was eventually repopulated (Gn 6:9).

It is likely that Noah, flood hero and vineyard planter, is really a composite of several figures from Hebrew tradition. This biblical Noah bears striking resemblance to a Mesopotamian deluge hero called *Ut-napishtim*. The entire biblical flood story is quite similar to the ancient Near East flood-legend in the famous *Epic of Gilgamesh*.

In the aftermath of the great deluge, God made a universal and everlasting covenant with Noah, his descendants, and all creatures of the earth (Gn 9:1-17). God promised that he would never again destroy the world with flood waters; a rainbow in the sky was the lasting sign of his holy covenant. With Noah God renewed the commands he had given at the time of creation. The episode of Noah reveals the human potential for sinfulness and evil, but it also shows that God continues his care and concern for the human race. The rainbow and the seasonal cycles of nature (Gn 8:20-22); offer hope and remind humans of God's intention to be faithful to his covenant relationship (Gn 8:20-22). (See also Covenant, Creation, Pentateuch.)

NOVENA is a nine-day period of devout prayer that uses set formulas of petition which are usually addressed to Mary or to one of the saints. Catholics make novenas to gain particular favors, especially when they have pressing and urgent needs. Novenas may be made publicly or privately.

Early Christians observed a Roman custom called the "novendialia," which was a nine-day period of sorrow and prayer after the death of a loved one. By the Middle Ages novenas had become prayerful nine-day preparations for important feasts such as Christmas. Eventually they became prayers of petition directed to the Blessed Virgin Mary and the saints.

Novenas are modeled after the apostles' nine days of prayer and waiting in the Upper Room. They prayed together for the gift of the Holy Spirit whom Jesus had promised to send. (The nine days stretch from Christ's Ascension into heaven until Pentecost Sunday.) Though novena prayers are believed to bring special favors and grace, they are not in any way better than other forms of prayer. (See also Indulgences, Pentecost, Prayer.)

OLD TESTAMENT is the portion of the bible that tells how God (Yahweh) first revealed himself to humankind, how he initiated a basic covenant relationship with his chosen people, the Hebrews, and how he set in motion a great plan for the salvation of the entire human race which was eventually fulfilled in Jesus Christ. The Old Testament is a collection of 46 books, written over a period of 900 years. The English term testament derives from the Latin *testamentum*, which means "covenant" or "agreement" in the biblical sense.

Some of the major events described in the Old Testament include the creation of the world; Moses leading the Hebrews out of slavery (the exodus and passover) to the promised land; the series of covenant agreements established between God and the chosen people; and the messages delivered to Israel by the prophets.

The Old Testament was compiled by many authors and editors, over a long period of time. It has three major parts: The Law—or Pentateuch—which has five books; the Prophets, which contains 21 books; and the Writings, which is a set of 13 books. The Catholic Church recognizes another set of seven books which scripture scholars call the deutero-canonicals. These are Tobit, Judith, Wisdom of Solomon, Ecclesiastes, Baruch, 1 Maccabees, and 2 Maccabees. This brings the Old Testament total to 46. Protestant Christians do not include the Deutero-canonical books in Protestant versions of the bible.

Catholics are taught that the Old Testament is an important collection of writings that should be read and studied. The Old Testament explains how God and his chosen people first entered into a covenant relationship. Though broken many times because of the sinfulness and weakness of the people, God remained faithful to the covenant. The Ten Commandments of God, basic norms that are the *foundation* of Christian morality, are in the Pentateuch section of the Old Testament. But most importantly the Old Testament reveals how God introduced his plan of salvation for all humans. The church teaches that the Old Testament must "remain permanently valuable" for Catholic Christians in all times and places. (See also Bible; Bible, Books of; Pentateuch.)

ORDERS is that sacrament of the church, through which men enter the ordained ministry. The word orders derives from the Latin *ordo*, which means "order" or "ranking." Through the sacrament of orders, church members are guaranteed that the gospel will be proclaimed, the sacraments celebrated, and their spiritual needs will be served. When conferring this sacrament the bishop imposes hands over the candidates, anoints them with oil (chrism), and prays that they might receive the gift of the Holy Spirit.

The New Testament does not present a clear model for leadership in the early church. There were numerous ministries: prophets, apostles, preachers, teachers, elders, administrators, deacons, and overseers. Ignatius of Antioch, in the year 111, wrote that the general practice was for bishops and presbyters (priest-like ministers) to preside at the eucharist. Ignatius added that without bishops, priests, and deacons the church community would not exist. By the end of the second century only those named by local bishops could preside at the Eucharist (the Mass), in their place. Previously various members of Christian communities were asked to preside as celebrants. About 230 A.D. Tertullian wrote about an *order* which applied to the clergy: this order had three categories of church ministers: bishop (the overseer), priest (the presbyter), and the deacon (the helper, server). The church did not have an official written declaration requiring ordination (in order to celebrate the eucharist) until 1208. Further decrees on this matter were made by the councils of Florence (1439) and Trent (1563).

These three degrees of orders have been reaffirmed in the church since Vatican Council II. The council noted that the ministerial priesthood is a sharing in the priesthood of the episcopate (the bishops), the authority of which rests in Jesus Christ himself. Priests are called to work with their bishops, to participate in the task of building up, sanctifying, and watching over (pastor-ing) the body of Christ and people of God, the church. The primary responsibility of priests—according to Vatican II—is proclaiming the good news of Christ through personal witness, missionary work, and catechesis (teaching). Candidates for ordination attend seminaries to prepare for this ministry.

The church teaches that men who are priests and bishops participate in the priestly, prophetic, and kingly offices of Jesus Christ. In the early 1970s the church issued a number of statements on the revised rites for ordination to the ministerial priesthood. The sacrament of orders may be received only once. The local bishop ordinarily administers the sacrament to men who have prepared for priesthood. In recent years the permanent diaconate has been renewed by the church. (There is also a transitional diaconate, for men who intend to become priests.) Some of the minor orders, for example, porter, exorcist, and subdeacon were terminated by Paul VI, in 1972. There are diocesan priests who receive orders from the local bishop and serve in his diocese, most often in a *parish* community. There are religious priests who are members of religious communities (for example, the Jesuits or the Franciscans), who are under the jurisdiction of religious superiors. These priests serve in many different capacities, and take the three vows of poverty, chastity, and obedience. (See also Bishop, Ministry, Sacrament.)

ORIGINAL SIN   is the condition or state into which every member of the human race is born. Every person is born into a world that is affected by sinfulness and each has an inclination to personal sin. Original sin (also called the sin of Adam) is the result of the selfish choice of the first humans to seek their own goals and desires rather than to do the will of the creator (God). Sin was thus introduced into the world.

In the book of Genesis the story of Adam and Eve illustrates how sinfulness became part of the human experience (2:15-17, 3:1-24), and how humans are responsible for sin. The term original sin is not in scripture. It was developed during the early centuries of the church. Theologians like Augustine and Thomas Aquinas wrote about the doctrine of original sin, while the Council of Trent (in 1547) formally taught that original sin came into the world through the sin of Adam and, thus, each human being inherits death and sinfulness. Yet Trent also noted that humanity is redeemed by Jesus even though it still suffers the effects of original sin.

The grace of God and salvation is offered to all persons through the saving deeds of Jesus Christ. Christians engage in a lifelong struggle to be open to God and to overcome the effects of sinfulness. Though they experience original sin's effects: self-centeredness, lack of respect for human life, racism, injustice, Christians can strive to love God and others, and to live in God's friendship.

Vatican Council II taught that through original sin humanity has inclinations toward evil. Freedom was abused and the original harmony between human beings and God was disrupted. As a result, much of human conduct is grounded in sinfulness (personal sin), and many human institutions/endeavors are hindered by sinful attitudes and values (social sin). This causes humanity to be estranged from God. The church points out that Jesus and Mary were the only two persons not born in original sin. Two important bible passages about original sin are found in Paul's epistles (1 Cor 15:21, and Rom 5:12–21). (See also Adam and Eve, Creation, Sin.)

PARISH   is a local community of Catholic Christians who share a common faith and participate in common worship and service. The term also refers to that geographical area of a diocese which is headed by a pastor who is under the jurisdiction of the bishop. The pastor is the spiritual leader of the parish as well as its administrator. He is appointed by the local bishop. In addition to the pastor many parishes also have associate pastors, who assist him in serving the needs of the people. In recent decades laypersons and religious have been given more active roles in leading the parish and sharing in the work of the community.

The word parish stems from the Greek *paroikos*, which means "dwelling near." Pastors and priests of parishes are not only leaders, they are also servants of the people of God, leading and serving parishioners as they hand on the teachings of the church, preside at worship, and represent Christ, especially in works of charity and compassion. Because of modern cultural pressures, many Catholics find that traditional large and formal parishes do not meet their needs. Some smaller community groups have developed, for example, communities modeled on the Hispanic *comunidades de base*. These groups are often designated "experimental."

Vatican Council II noted that qualified laypersons should help administer and lead the parish. In some places laity and religious meet regularly with the clergy to plan and evaluate parish activities. Laypersons serve on parish councils and committees. They also serve in ministry postions as DREs, coordinators, family ministers, evangelizers, youth ministers, special ministers, lectors, school principals, catechists, etc. Vatican II stressed that renewed efforts also must be made to encourage a living sense of community in parishes, especially through the celebration of the eucharist. (See also Community, Ecclesiology, Ministry.)

PAROUSIA   is a Greek word that means "presence" or "arrival." It refers to the second coming of the Lord Jesus at the end of time (the conclusion of salvation history) and the beginning of the perfected kingdom of God. That there will be a *parousia* is a doctrine of the church—based upon Christian hope.

The *parousia* is referred to a number of times in the bible. The gospels report that Jesus warned others to be watchful that he would return to earth, but only God the Father would know exactly when. Evidently the early Christians assumed that this second coming would occur very soon after Jesus' ascension to heaven. Saint Paul wrote that the *parousia* was indeed coming, but he warned Christians not to use it as an excuse to be lazy. The church has continued to teach that the *parousia* will signify the triumph of the Lord, that a general judgment of the living and the dead will take place, and the establishment of God's eternal Kingdom (through the transformation of the universe into a new dwelling and a new earth of justice and peace) will come about.

Recent biblical research on the gospels of Mark, Matthew, and Luke indicates that some of the images used by the evangelists have their source in the book of Daniel and in apocryphal writings. For example, Jesus is pictured as the Son of Man coming in glory with great power. The gospel of John also supposes a return of Christ; Jesus will come to take his followers to a place he has prepared. The second coming should be awaited in faith and hope, and not be feared or dreaded.

Through the doctrine of the second coming, the church reveals that the Christian message and way of life are hope-filled. During the Mass (right after the consecration of bread and wine), Catholics express their belief that Jesus will come again in glory. A branch of Catholic theology known as *Eschatology* is a study of "the last things"—the kingdom, heaven and hell, the second coming of Christ, the resurrection of the body, and the final judgment. The following biblical passages mention the parousia: Mt 24:3-14; Lk 21:27-29; Jn 14:13; Acts 1:11; 1 Cor 15:23; Ti 2:13; and 1 Thess 4:15-17. (See also Hope, Kingdom of God.)

PASCHAL CANDLE is a large candle that is blessed and lighted during Easter Vigil ceremonies in all Catholic churches. The Paschal Candle is a symbol of the risen Jesus and is kept in the sanctuaries of churches from Easter Sunday until the feast of the Ascension. It is lighted for most Masses during this 40-day period and is also lighted when the sacrament of baptism is celebrated.

On the front of the Paschal Candle are five large grains of incense arranged in the form of a cross. The five grains represent the five major wounds suffered by Jesus when he was crucified. At the top of the candle is an *Alpha* (beginning) sign and at the bottom is an *Omega* (end) sign which are meant to show that Jesus Christ is really the beginning and end of all that exists.

Also traced on the Paschal Candle, on the four sides of the cross, are numbers which indicate what year it is. (See also Candles, Holy Week, Sanctuary.)

PASCHAL LAMB is one of the many titles given to Jesus Christ.

The term paschal lamb comes from the scripture story about the exodus of the Jews from Egypt. According to God's instructions lambs were prepared and eaten by the Hebrew families on the night of their passover from slavery to freedom. According to the Law of Moses, special lambs were killed to celebrate the Hebrew passover and were eaten with bitter herbs and unleavened bread. This annual ceremony reminds the Jewish people of the quick and unpleasant journey out of Egypt.

Catholic Christians are urged to think of Jesus as a paschal lamb because he gave up his life for their salvation. Just as the Hebrews were saved from slavery in Egypt by Yahweh (God), the death of Jesus on the cross offers freedom to all from the slavery of sin. (See also Jesus, Titles of; Passover.)

PASSOVER is a seven-day Jewish festival, also known as the Pasch, during which Jewish people recall and celebrate how Yahweh helped the Hebrews escape from slavery in Egypt. The Passover feast begins on the 14th day of the Jewish month Nisan and centers on a special meal, the Seder supper.

The Seder meal originally included the eating of a young lamb sacrificed especially for the occasion. During the meal the story of the exodus from Egypt—called *Haggadah*—is read to those gathered at the table. Jewish people celebrate the Passover as a reminder that God's might secured their freedom from Egyptian tyranny. They also continue to celebrate it because they believe that God has commanded them to do so.

Jesus Christ was sacrificed—like the Passover lambs—in order that all of humanity might be freed from the slavery of sinfulness and evil. Catholics sometimes refer to Jesus as the "Lamb of God," and to his death and resurrection as the Paschal Mystery.

The first eucharist celebration took place on Holy Thursday at a Jewish Passover meal. This celebration is now referred to as the Last Supper of Jesus and his apostles. During the celebration Jesus asked something very special of his followers: he requested that they forever honor and remember his passover from death to new life through their celebration of the eucharist. As God had asked the Hebrews to always remember their passover from slavery to freedom so Jesus asks his followers to remember this new passover.

Note of Interest: No passover discussion would be complete without some mention of the "tenth plague" suffered by the Egyptians, as reported in the bible. On the night of the first Passover ritual meal, the Hebrews sprinkled some of the blood of the paschal lamb on their doorposts (Ex 12:21–32). The Lord came upon the land of Egypt and killed the firstborn male in every non-Hebrew household. Even the first son of Egypt's pharaoh was slain. But the Lord passed over the Hebrew homes, sparing their firstborn sons, because of the lamb's blood on their doorways. This event persuaded the pharaoh to let the Hebrews leave the land of Egypt where they were slaves. (See also Eucharist, Moses, Paschal Lamb.)

PAUL is the saint who is often called the Apostle to the Gentiles. He is best known by Catholics as the "author" of 14 epistles—or letters—which are in the New Testament. Paul was a Jew by birth, born into the tribe of Benjamin, but because his home city was Tarsus he was also a Roman citizen.

Paul was probably born about the same time as Jesus and was named Saul by his family. He studied the Old Testament, especially the Law of Moses in the Pentateuch. He became a Jewish lawyer and a Pharisee. He was also quite skilled as a tentmaker. Saul was very active in persecuting early followers of Jesus whom he believed were violating Jewish law. During a trip to the city of Damascus, Saul had a striking vision of the risen Jesus. After this experience he stopped persecuting the followers of Jesus. He became a convert to Christianity and began using the name Paul; he made at least three long missionary journeys to spread the good news of the gospel. He himself was often persecuted and he spent many months in prison. Paul was beheaded in Rome about 65 A.D. because of his faith in Christ.

Saint Paul traveled from Jerusalem to Rome and beyond in order to teach and preach about the salvation that Jesus offers to all persons. He founded many Christian communities, such as the one at Corinth. Paul's strong influence on the earliest Christian leaders helped them extend their missionary efforts to all the people in the world.

The Acts of the Apostles and Paul's epistles are the best sources to learn about his life and teachings. Although Paul was not one of the original 12 apostles, he still deserves the title "apostle to the gentiles." Saint Paul is one of the most important and most ingenious of the early church's leaders. The Catholic Church honors him on two feastdays, January 25th and June 29th. (See also Acts of the Apostles, Epistle.)

PAUL VI is the pope who followed John XXIII and preceded John Paul I. He was elected to the papacy on June 21, 1963, and he died 15 years later on August 6, 1978. Paul is remembered as the pope who presided over the second, third, and fourth major sessions of Vatican Council II. He was responsible for seeing that many council reforms were put into action throughout the universal church.

Paul's given name was Giovanni Battista Montini. He was born September 26, 1897 in northern Italy in the town of Concesio. After his schooling at Brescia, he prepared for the priesthood and was ordained on May 29, 1920. Four years later he began a tour of service with the Vatican's Secretariat of State that lasted for three decades. He served as Undersecretary from 1937 to 1954. In December 1954 Montini became Archbishop of Milan. He entered the College of Cardinals in December 1958.

Paul VI is remembered as the pope who reconvened Vatican II after John XXIII died. He formally issued or promulgated the landmark Vatican II documents and worked to assure that council reforms would be effected in the whole church.

Paul VI actively supported the ecumenical movement, the need for peace and justice in the world, reform and reorganization within church structures (including the Roman Curia), and the renewal of the church's liturgical practices. He promulgated the new Order of the Mass in 1969 and the revisions of the official liturgical calendar in 1970. He restored the permanent diaconate and called for lay ministries in the church. Paul VI is also remembered as the pope who canonized 84 persons (more than any other pope in history), and created 137 cardinals (also more than any other pontiff). He initiated reforms in the college of cardinals and established the on-going international synod of bishops. He is sometimes referred to as the "Pilgrim Pope," because of his extensive journeys. Paul was a diplomat and statesman who dialogued with powerful world leaders. He wrote seven encyclicals including *Humanae Vitae*, which condemned artificial birth control, abortion, and human sterilization. The encyclical *Populorum Progressio* centered on human dignity, basic rights, and social justice. (See also John XXIII, Vatican Council II.)

PENTATEUCH is one of the terms used to refer to the first books of the bible. The two other terms used are "the Law" and the *Torah*. The word Pentateuch is derived from the Greek *pentateuchos*, which means "the book of five volumes (or scrolls)." The Pentateuch is composed of these books: Genesis, Exodus, Leviticus, Numbers, and Deuteronomy.

For a long time it was thought that Moses was the author of the Pentateuch. In fact the Pentateuch was referred to as the "five books of Moses," and the "Mosaic Books." It is now known, thanks to the work of biblical researchers and historians, that the five books of the Pentateuch were edited into their present form long after the lifetime of Moses and only after centuries of oral and written development. The Pentateuch opens with accounts of the creation of the world and the earliest history of the human race. It then goes on to describe: God's call to Abraham and the other patriarchs; the call of Moses; the exodus of the Hebrews from oppression in Egypt; the covenant-relationship established between Yahweh and the Israelite people under Moses' guidance; the formation of the great Israelite nation. The Pentateuch also contains religious laws and guidelines for the Hebrew people.

The Pentateuch is a very significant portion of the Jewish bible; in fact, the Law as a whole is a central and sacred part of Jewish life and faith. Catholics and other Christians recognize that the Pentateuch describes their own roots in the Judaeo-Christian tradition, and of the old covenant which was fulfilled through the new covenant of Jesus Christ.

Following is a description of the five books of the Pentateuch.

Genesis describes the creation of the world and of the earliest members of the human race. It contains stories about the patriarchs, and describes the events that lead to enslavement of the people in Egypt.

Exodus describes the first passover meal of the Hebrews and the passing over from oppression to freedom, with Moses leading the Hebrew people. The story of the mosaic covenant and the development of the Israelites into a nation are also included.

Leviticus centers on Israel's holiness and on liturgical and worship requirements.

Numbers shows how the Israelites were organized and the role of authority in the Jewish nation.

Deuteronomy explains and describes the ways in which the Israelites should relate to each other and how the chosen people must relate to Yahweh. (See also Covenant, Creation, Moses.)

PENTECOST is celebrated fifty days after Easter in remembrance of the outpouring of the Holy Spirit on the first followers of Jesus. The story of the Pentecost-event is recorded in Acts of the Apostles in Chapter 2. The feast of Pentecost is often called the birthday of the church. The term itself is Greek and means "the 50th day."

Pentecost was originally a Jewish harvest festival that was held fifty days after Passover (Ex 34:22). The early Christians realized that the descent of the Spirit empowered Peter to boldly proclaim the good news of salvation in Jesus Christ. It empowered the followers of Jesus to baptize thousands gathered in Jerusalem for the Pentecost feast, and it enabled all of Christ's disciples to carry this good news to the whole world. First records of the Christian Pentecost feast date back to the 3rd century, but it is certain that Pentecost celebrations were held by the early church long before that time.

The Pentecost-event filled the followers of the risen Jesus with his Spirit and strengthened and encouraged them to fulfill the great mission they had received from him (Mt 28:16–20). In a sense they were really fired up and guided by the Holy Spirit to spread the gospel to all nations and to baptize believers. When the church celebrates Pentecost Catholics are reminded that the Spirit continues to guide Christ's followers and his church here on earth.

Catholics are taught that like the first Christians who received the Holy Spirit, they too have received the call to spread Christ's good news to all people. The feast of Pentecost is a moveable feast on the church's official calendar (it is not celebrated on the same date each year), and the feast remains a true celebration of the church's presence in the modern world, a community drawing closer and closer to perfection and to complete happiness with God. The sacrament of confirmation is sometimes referred to as personal Pentecost. Church leaders sometimes will refer to Pentecost as Whitsunday. Catholic devotions called novenas are compared to the nine-day period of intense prayer and waiting observed by Christ's followers before the Pentecost-event. (See also Confirmation, Easter, Liturgical Year.)

PEOPLE OF GOD   describes the community of faithful followers of Jesus Christ, the church. This term was popularized by Vatican Council II.

The nation of Israel was chosen by God (Yahweh), to be his chosen people. The Israelites (or Hebrews) thought of themselves as a unified people faithful to Yahweh (a corporate personality). The chief expression of this covenant relationship between Yahweh and his chosen people is found in the book of Exodus, 6:7-8. (Also see Lv 26:9-12.) Jesus Christ, the Son of God, established a new people of God, the community called church, and his earliest followers saw themselves as God's true chosen race, a holy nation, a people unified. (See 1 Pet 2:9-10).

The church uses the term "people of God" to symbolize that it is a single people, a true community that proclaims the good news of salvation. Its members are faithful to the teachings and commands of the Lord Jesus, seek and hope for the perfection of the kingdom of God (which has already begun), and seek to love and serve the whole of humanity and creation. All men and women are invited to join this community. Persons are initiated into this people of God through baptism. They celebrate the sacraments with other members, especially the eucharist, and the sacrament of reconciliation.

The unity of the new people of God has as its source the deep unity of the Father, Son, and Spirit, the Trinity. Vatican II taught that the church as people of God was founded by Jesus and remains the kingdom-on-earth (a messianic flock of priestly and prophetic people guided in a special way by Christ the Lord and his successors on earth). Vatican II also called the church a holy people and a dwelling-place of the Spirit, a unity of individuals who have true dignity and freedom, and a community of life, and truth, and love. The church calls believers to remain a faithful, worshipping body. The followers of Jesus sometimes characterized as the light of the world and salt of the earth—people who are instruments of salvation sent to extend and perfect the kingdom of God through love. (See also Church, Images of; Community, Ecclesiology.)

PETER   is one of the original 12 apostles of Jesus, the leader of the Christian community after the ascension of the Lord and a saint of the Catholic Church. The name Peter is derived from the Greek *petros*, which means "rock." Saint Peter is honored as the first pope and his true successors, the Bishops of Rome, have been the church's popes throughout the history of Christianity.

Peter's family name was actually Simon bar-Jonah (the

gospels note that he was renamed Peter by Jesus himself), and he came from the land of Galilee. The New Testament reports that he was a fisherman and that he was called at the same time as his brother Andrew to follow Jesus. Peter was married and lived in Capernaum. He appears in the Acts of the Apostles, but after Chapter 12 he is not mentioned again. The facts about the rest of his life are somewhat uncertain. It is generally thought that Peter made his way to the city of Rome where he was crucified (martyred) about 65 A.D.

The early Christian community depended on Peter for strong, authoritative leadership. He acted as leader at an important meeting of Christians (a council) in 52, in the city of Jerusalem. He was a bold spokesman for the early followers of Jesus. Peter is mentioned in the New Testament more often than any other apostle or disciple of Jesus. It has been traditionally believed that Peter lived, died, and was buried in Rome. Peter was probably buried at what is now the present site of St. Peter's Church in the Vatican.

Peter's authority to lead and guide the early Christians was received directly from Jesus Christ. His true successors, the Bishops of Rome, have the supreme authority to teach, govern, and guide the entire church. Two epistles (letters) of the New Testament bear Peter's name. There are two feast days on which Saint Peter is specially honored, February 22nd and June 29th.

Note of Interest: Two significant New Testament passages that indicate that Peter was meant by Jesus to be the head of the Christian community are Mt 16:17-19 and Jn 21:15-17. (See also Apostles, Pope.)

POPE is the successor of Saint Peter and supreme leader of the entire Catholic Church. The word pope can be traced both to the Latin *papa* and the Greek *pappas* which mean "father." The pope, or Holy Father as he is called, has the foremost authority in the church to teach on matters of faith and morals and to govern the members of the Catholic Church.

The New Testament indicates that Peter was a strong and trusted leader in the early church who was given special authority from Jesus to guide the other Christians (Mt 16:17-19, and Jn 21:15-17). Through the ages Peter's successors, the Bishops of Rome, have held the title pope and have faithfully proclaimed the gospel and guided the people of God.

The rules by which popes have been elected have changed a number of times over the centuries. In 1975 Paul VI revised papal election laws. He decreed that all cardinals under the age of 80 should come together in a conclave to choose a new pope whenever necessary. The pope is also called the Bishop of Rome, the Vicar of Christ, the Roman Pontiff, the Holy Father, and the Servant of the Servants of God. The term pontiff is used to denote that the pope is a kind of *bridge* that helps God and his people draw closer together. Like Saint Peter, the pope is a strong, trusted, spiritual leader, and a humble servant and shepherd. Because of his great authority Catholics and others are urged to listen to the pope with deep respect and obedience.

Building on scripture and many centuries of tradition, the church maintains that the pope holds supreme power in the church as its chief pastor. This doctrine on papal primacy was officially defined by Vatican Council I in 1870 and was reaffirmed by Vatican II. It is taught that though the pope may teach infallibly, without error, he most often unites in a spirit of collegiality with the other Catholic bishops in order to define teachings on faith and morals. There have been 265 popes, nine of whom have lived in the present century. Once a man is elected to the chair of Peter, he remains the pope for the rest of his life. The most recent popes include: Leo XIII, Pius X (who has been canonized a saint), Benedict XV, Pius XI, Pius XII, John XXIII, Paul VI, John Paul I, and John Paul II.

Note of Interest: At least 37 persons who had no right to the title or office have claimed to be the real pope. These people are known as "anti-popes." A church prayer for the pope (contained in the *Sacramentary*) refers to the pope as the "appointed successor to Saint Peter . . . the visible center and foundation of unity in faith and love." (See also Collegiality, Peter, Vatican Council I.)

PRAYER   is a communication with God and an awareness of his powerful, loving presence. Prayer can be silent or verbal, formal or informal, private or communal.

The four gospels report that Jesus prayed to the Father frequently and that he went off to quiet, deserted places to pray before crucial happenings in his life. The church describes prayer as the raising of one's heart and mind to God. There are four basic types of prayer: petition, adoration, thanksgiving, and contrition.

Prayer is openness to and communication with God, but it is also a dialogue initiated (given as a gift) by the Father. The prayerful person freely responds to God's offer to communicate; this response is one of faith and hope, a surrender to God's love. The response to God's initiative is like a hunger, a powerful longing to be with and converse with God.

There are many possible ways to pray: participation in the worship of the church (the liturgy—and in particular the eucharist, is the great communal prayer of believers); praying the Liturgy of the Hours (the divine office); joining bible study and prayer groups; quiet reflection alone or with others. Prayer of petition is asking prayer that centers on human needs. Prayer of adoration offers praise to God. Prayer of thanksgiving is full of gratitude, humility, and a sense of God's greatness. Prayer of contrition focuses on human failures and sinfulness but depends on God's ever-present offer of mercy and forgiveness to the sinner. In April 1980 Pope John Paul II said that prayer coupled with action "is at the base of the great enterprise of evangelization and of construction of the world according to God's plan."

Note of Interest: A retreat is a period of time used to step away from the routine activities of life. The individual retreatant (or a retreat group) seeks renewed peace and commitment to the Christian way through growth in faith, prayer, sacramental liturgy, scripture reading/meditation, and quiet reflection.

The practice of making retreats traces back to the wilderness experiences of biblical figures. Jesus himself spent time in the desert to reflect upon his ministry. Great saints like Ignatius Loyola, Francis de Sales, and Vincent de Paul also spent time in "desert prayer." In 1922 Pope Pius XI endorsed the opening of retreat houses for persons who wish to deepen their spirituality through retreat experiences. During the 1960s Vatican Council II urged Catholic bishops to stress the value of retreats for priests, religious, and laity. The council declared that periods of recollection and spiritual exercise renew and revitalize the activities of all witnesses to Christ. There are many kinds and forms of retreats: traditional silent retreats, youth retreats, parish renewals and missions, Cursillo, Charismatic Renewal, and Marriage Encounter retreats. (See also Charismatics, Worship.)

PRESENTATION   is the feast on which Catholics remember and honor the presentation of the infant Jesus at the temple in Jerusalem by Mary his mother and Joseph (Lk 2:22–38). Also commemorated on this feast is the purification of Mary (forty days after a child's birth: Lv 12:1–8). These events are celebrated on February 2nd. This feast was formerly called the Purification of the Blessed Virgin Mary and it was also known as Candlemas Day.

Jewish mothers were expected to participate in a purification rite, which was part of the Mosaic Law (the rules for this ritual are described in the books of Exodus and Leviticus in the Old Testament). For many years this feast was dedicated to Mary with emphasis on the purification, rather than on Jesus' presentation. Since 1969 the presentation has been emphasized. Since the 12th century, candles have been blessed on this feast to emphasize that Jesus Christ is the true light of the world. This is the reason the feast is sometimes called Candlemas Day.

Jesus is the savior who sheds light and offers salvation to a world that is troubled by sinfulness. During the blessing of the candles at Presentation feast ceremonies in 1979, Pope John Paul II expressed the hope that the special candles would remain symbols of the light of the world that is Christ. (See also Candles, Holy Family.)

PROPHET is a person called by God to deliver divinely revealed messages to humankind. The statements and symbolic actions of the biblical prophets often centered on hopes, promises, and warnings about the covenant established between God (*Yahweh*) and his chosen people. In a sense biblical prophets read the signs of the times and constantly called the Hebrews to be faithful to their relationship with Yahweh. Our word prophet has Greek origins which mean "one who speaks before others."

The most important Old Testament prophets lived between 900 and 500 B.C.; this significant period of prophetic activity ended when the Israelites were freed from Babylonian captivity in 538. After the time of the prophets, the Hebrew people were guided more by God's revelation in the written law rather than by the words of the prophets. God truly spoke through the prophets to the nation of Israel and his Spirit inspired the prophets to perform their ministry. It is traditionally believed by the Jews that some of the prophets suffered persecution and some even died at the hands of their enemies.

John the Baptist, a kinsman of Jesus who announced the coming of the kingdom of God, was a prophetic figure in New Testament times. Jesus too was considered a great prophet by some people of his time but it seems he never specifically claimed to be a prophet. New Testament writings suggest that the church of the first century did indeed have prophets; Paul noted in his epistles that prophecy is a special gift from God.

There were three major Old Testament prophets: Isaiah, Jeremiah, and Ezekiel, and a number of minor prophets, such as Amos, Hosea, Joel, Micah, Baruch, and Zechariah. Portions of the biblical books of the prophets are frequently read at Mass and at other special liturgies. (See also Bible, Old Testament, Revelation.)

PURGATORY is that state or condition into which souls enter to be cleansed or purified from the effects of unforgiven sin or to endure temporal punishment for sins already forgiven. Souls in purgatory are considered not yet worthy of heavenly happiness. The word purgatory is based on a Latin term that means cleansing.

Early Christians prayed for those who had gone to a "place of tears" after death. The actual word "purgatory" has been used by church members since the Middle Ages. The Councils of Lyons (1274) and Florence (1439) taught that souls in purgatory need the prayers and good works of those who still live on earth. The Council of Trent (16th century) stated that offering prayers and especially the eucharist for the sake of those in purgatory greatly helps those souls.

The church's belief in purgatory is centered in Catholic tradition (there is no clear biblical basis for the doctrine of purgatory). It has been traditionally taught that the souls in purgatory are the souls of persons who have died in the state of grace, but who have not perfectly atoned for their sins. They must undergo a process of painful separation from God but they do experience a deep sense of hope and joy as they prepare for complete happiness in heaven. One line of theological thinking holds that these souls still cling in some ways to human failings and thus cannot fully enjoy unity with God.

Catholics believe that the souls in purgatory are happy since they are assured of heaven and the beatific vision of God. The process of pain and separation from God which the souls endure has sometimes been compared to a burning fire. According to the church teaching, their suffering may be lessened by the prayers, works of charity, and reception of the eucharist offered for them by believers on earth. (See also Heaven; Saints, Communion of; Sin.)

RACHEL   was the second wife of Jacob, a man who was one of Israel's three great patriarchs. She was the mother of Joseph and Benjamin, two of Jacob's 12 sons.

Rachel was a shepherdess, the younger daughter of a man named Laban (Gn 29). Jacob met her when he began to work for Laban. He received a promise from Laban that he could marry Rachel after working for seven years. However, Laban tricked Jacob into marrying Rachel's sister, Leah. Another agreement was finally reached between Jacob and Laban: if Jacob worked hard for seven more years, he could then marry Rachel. Jacob agreed to the bargain and eventually Rachel and Jacob were married.

Rachel and Jacob lived about 1700 years before Christ. It is generally held that Rachel died soon after giving birth to Benjamin, her second son. It is an old tradition that she was buried at Ephrath, north of the city of Jerusalem. Jacob's years of hard labor to win Rachel as his wife indicate that she was a good and faithful woman. (See also Jacob, Joseph [Son of Jacob], Old Testament.)

RECONCILIATION is one of the seven sacraments of the church. Sometimes this sacrament is called penance and/or confession. The word reconciliation refers to the healing of the rift between a sinful human being and God and others in the community. The word penance, which comes from the Latin *poenitentia*, means "contrition" and "repentance for wrongdoing." Through the sacrament of reconciliation sinful persons are reconciled to the loving and merciful God and to the church community. To receive forgiveness through this sacrament, one must have true sorrow, be willing to confess the sins to a priest, make reparation for sin, and receive absolution. The words used by the priest to absolve (forgive) sins are "I absolve you from your sins in the name of the Father, and of the Son, and of the Holy Spirit."

A New Testament basis for the sacrament of reconciliation is found in Jn 20:22-23. Christians believe that Jesus cared about sinners and called all persons to convert (turn away) from sin and evil. The apostles preached that sin could be forgiven and that salvation was offered to humanity through Jesus the messiah. In the sixth century, severe public penances were administered for sins of murder, heresy, and adultery. Lesser penances, such as fasting, prayer, charitable works, were assigned for less grievous sins. During this period Christians could receive the sacrament only once in a lifetime. By the 7th century, however, they were able to confess sinfulness more frequently—to a bishop or priest who acted more as a judge than a healer or reconciler. The penances assigned became a strictly private matter. Emphasis was placed on listings/codings of various penances to be assigned for the many kinds of sins. By the fourteenth century great stress was placed on making satisfaction for sins. Belief that penance was a sacrament of reconciliation between the sinner, God, and the church community had waned. The Council of Florence (1439) formally declared that penance was one of the seven sacraments and that to be forgiven one must have contrition, confess to a priest, and make satisfaction by doing a penance. In 1551 the Council of Trent noted that this sacrament was instituted by Christ and is distinct from baptism.

In recent decades the belief that penance is a means of reconciliation has been restored. Through this sacrament the mercy of

God is extended to the individual sinner, yet through its celebration the entire people of God comes to recognize that it is in need of God's grace, and that it must also undergo the process of daily conversion. Vatican Council II called for a revision of the rite of this sacrament, saying that is aids Christians in their desire for ongoing conversion to authentic Christian living.

The church continues to teach that the usual minister of the sacrament of reconciliation is a priest or bishop. Since 1974 (with the publication of the *Ordo Paenitentiae*), the church has provided three forms for the celebration of reconciliation: general absolution (does not require private confession and is used infrequently), 2) communal penance service (including a liturgy of the word and individual confession/absolution), and 3) traditional private confessions and absolution. The church stresses that this sacrament is a means of grace and that (in most cases) expression of contrition, confession of all mortal sins, and some type of reparation/satisfaction are necessary for forgiveness.

Note of Interest: The main elements of the revised ritual for the sacrament of reconciliation include: welcome by the minister, scripture reading (optional), confession of sin by the penitent, prayer for forgiveness (statement of contrition), absolution, praise/prayer of thanksgiving, conclusion/dismissal of the penitent.

The 1983 6th General International Synod of Bishops has as its theme: Reconciliation and Penance in the Mission of the Church. (See also Actual Sin, Conversion, Sacrament.)

REDEMPTION   is the process by which humanity is bought back through Jesus Christ's saving deeds into God's life of grace. Catholics believe that Jesus is the redeemer, the one who offers freedom from sin and shows the way to eternal salvation. It is fundamental to Christianity that redemption has occurred through Jesus' works, yet the world awaits a final redemption-to-come—a conversion of all creation from sin and selfishness to the goodness of God and his perfected kingdom.

The teaching of the church is that Jesus ransomed humankind from slavery to sin, that he was the Son of God and savior who proclaimed the good news of the kingdom, called others to conversion and faith, and reconciled the world to himself and the Father (2 Cor 5:19; Rom 5:15-19). During the Middle Ages the church emphasized that Jesus was a holy redeemer who was sacrificed on the cross for the sins of all people. The term Paschal Mystery was used to describe the redemption brought about by Jesus through his passion, death, and resurrection.

Redemption and salvation are offered to every member of the human race through Jesus' saving deeds and the outpouring of his Spirit. These gifts are offered and people are free to accept or reject them. The redeeming work of Christ is not accepted by all. Yet humanity has been redeemed from sin and evil. Human beings have been redeemed to offer responsible, Christian service to the world in order to improve it and to bring about the perfected kingdom, and for a free and full response to God in faith and hope.

The Catholic Church teaches that Jesus Christ was made man in order to redeem and save all human beings. He was sent by God to establish the kingdom-on-earth. The church—the sacrament of salvation—exists so that the kingdom may fully come and to help the human race on the journey toward salvation. The branch of Catholic theology called *Soteriology* is the study of salvation, which centers on Jesus Christ's suffering, death, resurrection, and exaltation by God. (See also Christology, Salvation.)

RELIGIOUS ORDERS   are communities of individual Christians who seek to live as active witnesses to the good news of Jesus Christ, and who have pledged to observe the vows of poverty, chastity, and obedience. Persons who enter religious life are called sisters or nuns, brothers, or religious priests. Religious orders follow specific ways of living and rules for life that help them offer Christian service to the church and to humankind.

In the 3rd century some men in the Middle East went to the desert to lead solitary lives of prayer and on-going conversion. These hermits soon had many followers. Eventually some of these followers banded together to form religious communities. This development led to the rise of community-oriented monasticism—a lifestyle that stressed community living, prayer, reflection, and solitude. Those who chose to live the monastic life in monasteries were influenced by the *Rule of St. Benedict*, which dates to the 6th century. Formal religious orders began to emerge in the 11th century. In succeeding centuries members of religious orders turned more toward the church as a whole and the secular world to offer genuine Christian service to others.

Men and women who live in religious communities are supposed to be living reminders that Jesus Christ is present in his church. Some men who prepare for the priesthood choose to join a religious order, to live in a religious community, and observe the evangelical counsels of poverty, chasitity and obedience. These men are called "ordered priests" or "religious priests." Religions must undergo a substantial period of study and training to prepare for such ministries as catechesis, teaching, nursing, social work, pastoral counselling, etc. Vatican Council II called for renewal of religious life in its *Decree on the Appropriate Renewal of Religious Life (Perfectae Caritatis)*. This renewal should center on the original inspiration of each Order and involves adjustment to the changing circumstances of modern life. Pope Paul VI (in August 1966) issued sweeping guidelines for the renewal of religious life in *Ecclesiae Sanctae*.

Some religious orders embrace a contemplative life. Contacts outside the order are kept to a minimum, since they focus on prayer, penance and solitude. Other religious communities also offer active service, to help build the kingdom of God.

Vatican II taught that observing the evangelical counsels is an answer to "a divine call to live for God alone not only by dying to sin but also by renouncing the standards of the world. [Religious] have handed over their entire lives to God's service in an act of special consecration which is deeply rooted in their baptismal consecration and which provides an ampler manifestation of it." (See also Celibacy, Ministry, Vows.)

RESURRECTION   is the event which is the heart and core of all Christian belief. At the resurrection Jesus Christ was raised to new life and entered a victorious, glorified state. The church explains that Jesus died, was raised from the dead, has ascended to the Father, and will come back at the end of time. The resurrection is celebrated on Easter Sunday, which is the high point of the church's liturgical year.

All four gospel versions in the New Testament note that Jesus really died and really returned to life. The New Testament reports that the risen Jesus appeared to the apostles and to other followers. He "ascended" to heaven, after which his community of followers awaited the sending of his Spirit. Christians have believed over the many centuries that Jesus was not only raised from the dead; he was also transformed (his body was glorified) as well. The church has taught that the resurrection is at the very center and the heart of her preaching and teaching.

Belief in the resurrection and faith in the good news of salvation impelled the early Christians to spread the gospel, baptize, and preach that Jesus Christ, through his Spirit, was living and present within the community of his followers. Because of the resurrection, Christians proclaimed the divinity of Jesus. Once the church began to fully comprehend the meaning of Jesus' resurrection, its members were transformed into hope-filled, committed bearers of his message. Some theological speculation centers on the event called the resurrection. Since there were no known eyewitnesses to the raising of Jesus, it has been suggested that the resurrection is not an historical event but rather a *transhistorical* event—something that occurred beyond the limits of time and space, and so is beyond what we usually define as an actual historical event.

The Catholic Church maintains that belief in the resurrection of Jesus is fundamental and at the very center of Christianity. It teaches that the crucified Lord Jesus was raised from the dead and glorified, and that by his holy resurrection all who have faith can be raised to life and glory with him forever. The church offers baptism to all and calls all human beings to belief in Christ, so that all men and women can share in the new life of the resurrected Lord. The Spirit could not have been sent to the community of believers unless Jesus was raised and glorified. The church teaches that Catholics participate in the death and resurrection of Christ when they celebrate the eucharist and in looking forward to his return in glory with the parousia.

Some significant passages in the New Testament mention the resurrection. These include: Mk 16:1–8, 9–20; Mt 28:1–28; Lk 24:1–53; Jn 20:1–29, 21:1–23; Acts 2:14–36, 3:12–26, 4:8–12, 5:29–32, 10:34–43; Rom 1:1–5, 8:34, 10:8–9; 1 Cor 12:3, 15:3–5; 1 Thess 1:9–10; Phil 2:6–11; Col 1:15–20; Eph 1:20–22; 1 Pet 1:18–22; Heb 1:3–4. (See also Easter, Faith, Miracles.)

REVELATION   is God's free and loving self-communication especially through Jesus Christ his son but also through his deeds, through other persons, and through his words. This good news of salvation has been continually proclaimed and handed on by Christ's faithful followers in the church. The word revelation stems from the Latin *revelatio*, which means "unveiling" or "uncovering."

God has revealed himself, and thus has "given" himself to his people in many ways throughout history. He is revealed through creation, through the words and actions of human beings, through events in history, and through the entire church, the community of God's new people.

The Council of Trent taught that there are two sources of divine revelation: scripture and tradition. Vatican Council II clarified that there is but one divine source (or stream) of revelation, and scripture and tradition are the two forms by which God's revelation is proclaimed. Vatican II also taught that believers must be aware of the signs of the times to understand how the Holy Spirit continues to work in the world: through the experiences of men and women, through other religious traditions, through all the events of contemporary times. These signs have to be interpreted and understood in terms of the gospel message. In this sense revelation can be viewed as an ongoing *process* as opposed to something finished and complete. The fullness of God's self-disclosure has been presented irrevocably to humankind in history, but God continues to offer the gift of himself.

The church teaches that divinely revealed truth originates in God's perfect, loving goodness and wisdom, Through his words and deeds, Jesus Christ fulfilled and perfected God's self-communication in salvation history. Through scripture and the church's sacred tradition, divine revelation is handed on to believers, and God continues to dwell with his people. Revelation and faith are like partners: People hear God's revelation and re-spond in faith to this great self-communication with trust in their God. (See also Bible, Faith, Inspiration, Tradition.)

ROSARY is a prayer devotion in honor of Mary practiced by a number of Catholics. Rosary beads are used to pray decades of the Hail Mary. An Our Father opens each decade and a Glory Be prayer closes each. The rosary can be prayed aloud or silently while meditating on the joyful, sorrowful, and glorious mysteries (events recalled from the lives of Jesus and Mary). In the United States the rosary is begun with the Apostles Creed, an Our Father, three Hail Mary prayers, and one Glory Be. After the five or more decades have been said, the Hail Holy Queen prayer is recited and sometimes also the prayer of the Feast of the Rosary.

The type of rosary most Catholics use is the Dominican Rosary. Saint Dominic received this particular rosary from the Blessed Virgin Mary (this Catholic tradition can be traced to Alan de la Roche who lived during the 15th century). With the establish-ment of an official rosary confraternity, plus the granting of numerous indulgences by many popes, the praying of the rosary became a highly popular devotion. By 1573 an official feast of the rosary was declared and made part of the church's liturgical life.

There is some question about the origin of the rosary. The claim that Saint Dominic received it during an actual appearance of the Blessed Virgin has been disputed. Whatever its origin many who pray the rosary believe that it is a valid, meditative type of prayer.

Many popes have encouraged Catholics to pray the rosary. In recent decades Pius XI granted a full (plenary) indulgence to all who pray the rosary before the blessed sacrament. Pius XII recom-mended that Catholics pray the rosary devoutly and often. In the United States the church supports a Rosary Altar Society, based in New York, which is an extension of the rosary confraternity in this country. The feast of Our Lady of the Rosary was permanently placed on the church's official liturgical calendar in 1716; this feast is celebrated on October 7th. (See also Mary, Prayer, Sacramentals.)

RUTH   is an Old Testament figure, a Moabite woman who married Boaz and thus became a member of the Israelite people. She had a son named Obed who was the grandfather of King David. She was therefore the great-grandmother of King David. Her story is told in the book of Ruth in the Old Testament.

It is not known who actually wrote the book of Ruth or precisely when it was written. One good process for dating it places the compostion sometime just before or after the 8th century B.C., however this date remains uncertain.

Ruth's story is possibly a well-written piece of fiction. But it appears that the tradition that Ruth's son Obed was the father of Jesse, who in turn was the father of David, is correct. It was from Ruth's family line—"from the house of David" and from "the root of Jesse"—that Jesus Christ was born in the town of Bethlehem.

The book of Ruth stresses that people ought to place their complete trust in Yahweh (God) and continue to believe that it is hc who offers salvation to all who have faith in him. (See also Bible, Books of; David, king; Old Testament.)

SACRAMENTALS   are blessed objects, prayers, or blessings which are identified by the church as sacred in a unique way (sacred in the sense of the Latin word *sacrare*, "to be set apart" or consecrated for a special purpose). Catholic sacramentals include the bible, holy water, medals, the rosary, the sign of the cross, blessed palm, ashes (on Ash Wednesday), the crucifix, chrism (oil for anointing), candles, holy pictures, statues, the way of the cross, the office (Liturgy of the Hours), and more.

Some sacramentals were called sacraments before the church formally defined that there are only seven sacraments: baptism, confirmation, eucharist, penance, anointing, orders, and matrimony. This was defined by the Council of Trent (1547), and the preceding Councils of Lyons II (1274), and Florence (1439).

Sacramentals are sacred signs that help church members recognize that Christ is always with them. Vatican Council II noted that the sacramentals bear a resemblance to the sacraments: they signify effects, particularly of a spiritual kind, which are obtained through the church's intercession. Through sacramentals Catholics are disposed to receive the chief effect of the sacraments

(God's grace), and some occasions of life are made more holy. (See also Grace, Sacrament.)

SACRAMENTS are sacred, visible signs of God's presence, which manifest the faith of the church and through which God's free gift of grace is offered. Jesus Christ is *the* greatest sacrament, the sign of the encounter between the unseen God and humans. The church is a universal sacrament of salvation for all people. The word sacrament comes from two Latin words: *sacramentum*, "solemn obligation," and *sacrare*, "to set apart as holy, sacred."Since the Middle Ages, the church has maintained that there are seven sacraments: baptism, confirmation, eucharist, reconciliation, matrimony, orders, and anointing of the sick.

Since ancient times people have used special rituals and symbols to signify their belief in something greater than themselves. Jesus used symbols and ceremonies to express his unique relationship with his heavenly Father. The church has always taught that Jesus, as the founder of the church, instituted the sacraments, the signs of salvation. Saint Augustine defined sacrament as a "visible sign of invisible grace." Thomas Aquinas (in the 13th century) taught that a sacramental sign expresses the faith of those who receive it, expresses true worship of the divine, indicates the true unity and faith of the entire church body, and exists as an effective sign of God's (and Christ's) presence among humans. Over the centuries, sacraments were sometimes considered "magic" actions that cause grace. But the church teaches that sacramental signs do not have any magical effects. Sacraments are free gifts made by God to human beings. By receiving the sacraments people freely choose to accept this divine self-communication and respond to God in faith. The official decision that there are seven sacraments was made at the Council of Trent in 1547. Previous statements to this effect were made at the Second Council of Lyons (1274), and Council of Florence (1439). For well over 1000 years, the church functioned without this definition of the exact number of sacraments. In fact many sacred rituals were used in earlier centuries. These are now called sacramentals.

The belief that sacraments are special, grace-filled encounters between God and humans has received much emphasis recently among church theologians and teachers. In each sacramental action believers truly meet Jesus in an intimate way and are joined closer to him. Through the sacraments they celebrate their own faith-stories and the faith-story of Christ's community. Each sacramental action helps to make the church's members more like Jesus who centered on doing the Father's will as he prepared for the kingdom-to-come. The New Testament clearly distinguishes two sacraments (baptism and the eucharist), while church tradition maintains that confirmation, reconciliation, matrimony, orders, and anointing of the sick are also sacraments. Since the 16th century, Protestant Christians have disputed the church's claim to seven sacraments. Some recent ecumenical dialogues have centered on this matter and have led to some statements about the various sacramental signs.

Jesus Christ is the ultimate sacrament, the sign of the encounter between God and humans, and the principal minister of all sacraments. The church is a universal sacrament of salvation for the entire people of God. The seven sacraments are visible signs of the church's living faith. Vatican Council II taught that the purpose of the sacraments is to sanctify people, thus building up the body of Christ. The seven sacraments are signs of faith-filled life in Christ, and so presuppose active faith. But they also nourish, strengthen, and express faith. Vatican II made special mention of the eucharist as a sacrament of faith and a sacred mystery most significant for the spiritual good of individuals and for the whole people of God. (See also Grace, Holiness, Worship.)

SACRISTY is a room in the church where vestments and other items used in Catholic worship (chalice, candles, ciboria, hosts and wine, cruets, monstrance, etc.) are kept. Those involved as ministers in the eucharistic celebration (the Mass) often vest in the sacristy. The word sacristy derives from two Latin words: *sacristia* and *sacrum*. Both mean "sacred," or "holy."

SAINTS, COMMUNION OF is the community of the entire people of God. This communion of saints includes those in heaven, the members being purified in Purgatory, and the faithful on earth.

Early followers of Christ (Saint Paul, for example) sometimes referred to other Christians as saints, but eventually the word saints applied only to those in heaven. The term "communion of saints" is found in the Apostles' Creed, a statement of faith that dates back to the early centuries of the church. This "communion" originally signified the fellowship and salvation shared by God's people. Later it came to mean the relationship shared by those on earth, in purgatory, and in heaven. These three groups have been called the church militant, church suffering, and church triumphant. The church teaches that the saints in heaven can intercede on behalf of those on earth (these saints are often prayed to for help). Members of the communion on earth can help those being purified through prayer and good works. The church has traditionally taught that everyone in heaven is a saint—not just those who have been canonized.

The communion of saints has been recognized in recent decades by Vatican Council II and by Pope Paul VI (in his *Credo of the People of God* and in a 1967 statement, *Indulgentiarum Doctrina*). Vatican II held that the worship of those on earth is enriched by participation in the communion of saints; the union of all members of the people of God—living and dead—is remembered and celebrated in the Mass. Because they believe in the communion of saints, Catholics honor the saints, pray for and do acts of charity for the dead in purgatory, and hope for the completion of the communion at the second coming of Jesus, in the perfected kingdom-coming. (See also Canonization, Heaven, Purgatory.)

SALVATION   means permanent union with God and all those others who are united in him. The salvation of all humanity is the goal of Jesus Christ's redeeming work. Salvation is a gift from God, freely offered and meant to be freely accepted. No one can earn or gain eternal salvation on his or her own. The word salvation comes for the Latin *salus*, "health."

One should look for personal salvation (unending union with God in the future) after death, but also should seek, through love of God and neighbor and service to humankind, salvation for all. This ultimate salvation will include the perfected kingdom of God (and full union with his people), an end to human sinfulness, and the everlasting and happy life of the world to come for which Christians pray. The church has been called the universal "sacrament of salvation" on earth (by Vatican II).

Note of Interest: Sometimes Catholics speak about "salvation history." This is the story of God's efforts to lead humanity toward the perfected kingdom and eternal salvation and happiness in his presence. Salvation history includes the creation, the events of Old Testament times, Jesus Christ—God's supreme revelation, the mission/history of the church, and the parousia. (See also Grace, Kingdom of God, Redemption.)

SANCTUARY   is the area in Catholic churches where the altar is placed. In the sanctuary priests and bishops lead the church community in prayer, and preside at and celebrate the Mass (the eucharist). The Word of God is proclaimed in the sanctuary by members of the congregation, called readers or lectors.

Traditionally the sanctuary was divided from the rest of the church by being elevated in some way or by a communion rail. In general accord with the renewal of the liturgy since Vatican Council II, the sanctuary area and altar have been situated more to the center (the midst) of the worshipping community, rather than to one end or one side of the church's interior.

The word sanctuary comes from the Latin *sanctuarium*, a "holy place," a shrine.

SAUL was the first king of the nation of Israel. It is believed that King Saul ruled for 20 years, from 1020 to 1000 B.C.—and was very much admired and respected as a gifted leader.

Saul was born into the tribe of Benjamin and was the son of Cis. He and his wife had several children, both sons and daughters, but he also had several children by other women. When the Israelites were endangered by their enemies the Philistines, the people realized that they would need a strong leader who could help and protect them. Saul was then a member of Israel's military forces and he was chosen to be their first king.

King Saul was a great warrior, but he was also a very moody man. A young Israelite named David was called into Saul's house to play harp music to calm the leader. David became very popular with the Israelite people when he defeated the greatest Philistine warrior, Goliath. Saul became very jealous of David. In fact he tried to have David killed even though the young man had married one of the king's own daughters.

Even though Saul had great abilities as a military man and as king of Israel, he sometimes failed to show proper love and respect for Israel's God, Yahweh. It is probable that Saul's intense emotions—including his strong desire to kill David—led to two important events in Jewish and Christian history: 1) Saul killed himself (committed suicide) during a battle with the Philistines; 2) his death was a major turning point that opened the way for David to become the next king. (See also David, King; Old Testament; Solomon.)

SIN is the conscious turning away from God's loving offer of friendship that leads to a weakening or total breakdown of our relationship with him and our relationship with others. Sinfulness from a biblical perspective means to miss the mark. Through sin a man or woman fails to respond to God's offer of love and friendship. The word sin comes from the Old English *syn*.

Although it is not known exactly how sin became part of the human condition, the story of Adam and Eve in the book of

Genesis explains that human beings freely chose sinfulness, and that God is not responsible for it. The Old Testament describes sin as the failure to live by the covenant established between Yahweh and his chosen people. The gospels recognize that sin is a real threat to humanity's good and that Jesus, the promised messiah, has overcome sin through his life, death, and resurrection. In his writings Saint Paul emphasized that believers die to sin through Jesus rather than through observing the older law of Moses. Over the centuries the church defined the two kinds or classes of sin—mortal and venial— which can be forgiven in the sacrament of reconciliation. Mortal sin involves full consent of the will, sufficient reflection, and serious matter. The sin of Adam, the effects of which all men and women suffer, is called Original Sin.

For a long time sin was considered a transgression (a breaking) of the law of God. More recently theologians have described sinfulness as a weakening of or complete turning away from a personal relationship with God. Sin is failure to respond to God's great love. Emphasis is placed on the attitudes and motives of the sinful person not so much on the actual deed or the rule broken. Sin can be personal and social. Personal sin is freely committed by responsible persons; social sin is evil which creeps into entire organizations, structures, communities, or societies. It harms individuals as well as whole communities. Christians are challenged to actively combat social sin.

Sin is both a reality and a mystery: it is an undeniable reality in the lives of human beings; it is a mystery in that no definition or phrase fully sums up or expresses just what it really is. The Christian life is one of ongoing conversion away from sinfulness and self-centeredness toward acceptance (through Christ) of God's loving offer of friendship. The church seeks to help men and women to live as mature, loving Christians. Sinfulness must be viewed within the context of a person's whole life. Is that life fundamentally Christian or un-Christian in its entirety? The church teaches above all that God is merciful and that he loves sinners and will always forgive sin if the person is truly sorry.

Note of Interest: Some theologians classify sin as mortal, serious, and venial. Moral sin is a total break with God, signifying a "fundamental option" for evil. In some cases a single action can be mortally sinful, but more usually one deed does not constitute mortal sin. Serious sin is a reflection of evil tendencies in a human being which threaten to lead to a total break with God, but which do not in themselves do so. Venial sin is a refusal or failure to love God, others, and self—a decision not to grow as a Christian, venial sin does not usually stop the conversion process or end one's "fundamental option" to love God and live the Christian life. (See also Actual Sin, Original Sin, Reconciliation.)

SOCIAL JUSTICE   is basic respect for human beings coupled with concern for and action on behalf of human rights. Pope John XXIII, declared in 1961 that human beings are the cause, foundation, and reason why all social institutions exist. The church affirms and defends the ultimate dignity and rights of every human person.

Social justice means the total ongoing effort to proclaim and live the gospel command to love God and neighbor. It is an active effort to reform societies, governments, institutions, and structures that deny the basic rights of human beings. Catholic teaching on social justice stems from the words and deeds of the Hebrew prophets but especially from the ministry of Jesus Christ. Catholic social doctrine has made great strides since the late 19th century, when Leo XIII was pope. Since then a number of important social teachings, encyclicals and synodal statements, for example have been handed on to the Catholics of the world.

The church teaches that the drive for justice in the world is at the very center of Christian existence. It is a constitutive element of church life. The newer developments of technology, social institutions and structures, and the media have great potential for good but can be used for evil purposes and for harm to human beings. The cause of social justice seeks to make the world aware of how humanity can best be served by its many products.

The encyclicals of the church that have dealt with social justice include: *Rerum Novarum* (1891), *Quadregesimo Anno* (1931), *Mater et Magistra* (1961), and *Pacem in Terris* (1963). Vatican Council II's Constitution on the Church in the Modern World (*Gaudium et Spes*, 1976), spoke of the need for social justice, as did Pope Paul VI's 1967 encyclical, *Populorum Progressio*. John Paul II has said that he seeks basic human rights and an end to oppression on earth. Pope John XXIII called for recognition of the rights and dignity of individuals, and noted that the Christian ministry of social justice includes care for the poor and destitute, help for underdeveloped nations, and the search for freedom, peace, and humane living conditions for all. (See also Charity, Morality, Works of Mercy.)

SOLOMON   the third King of Israel, was the son of David and his wife Bathsheba. Solomon is remembered as a very wise man who ruled the Israelite nation from about 960 to 922 B.C.

Solomon's reign was a peaceful one. He was able to expand the power, wealth, and territory of Israel. Much has been written about his reign in the Old Testament, especially in the second book of Chronicles, which notes that he assumed firm control of the kingdom when his father, David, died.

Solomon was intelligent, cultured, and capable of great wisdom in his actions and decisions. Some scholars believe that he wrote parts of the book of Proverbs. Solomon was named Jeddidiah when he was born, but he took the name Solomon when he became the King of Israel.

Though he was a wise and great leader who eventually built a temple for the chosen people, Solomon was also a weak man who was anxious for power, money, and pleasure. His extravagances aroused Yahweh's displeasure and probably contributed the eventual division of Israel after his death. Despite his numerous shortcomings Solomon is respected as a man of wisdom and as a king of Israel who led the nation in peace. (See also David, King; Old Testament; Saul.)

SUICIDE   is the intentional taking of one's own life. The term has two Latin roots, *sui* and *cidium*, which mean "self-killing." The church teaches that willful suicide is a violation of the 5th Commandment since only God the creator can decide how long a person should live.

While the church has traditionally condemned suicide it nevertheless recognizes that suicide is often the result of human desperation and despair. The church has always honored and upheld the belief that a Christian may sacrifice his or her life for a good cause, such as the "laying down of one's life for one's friend," (Jn 15:13).

Suicide (as well as abortion, euthanasia, and murder) is a violation of the right to life. Suicide and suicide-attempts can often be prevented through proper care for and treatment of the suicidal person. This is a problem that affects all age groups and all echelons of society. Some of the things that may lead to suicide include: problems that seem overwhelming, stress and anxiety, depression, life crisis, drug dependency, old age, and sickness. Support and encouragement from others, as well as professional help, often help suicidal persons. The church recognizes that suicide causes tremendous suffering in families and also harms the entire community within which the victim lived. Repeated, serious failure to care for one's own health and general well-being is sometimes considered suicidal.

In May 1980, Pope John Paul II stated that no one may dispose of life at will since life is a precious gift from God. He taught that intentionally causing one's own death, or suicide, is as wrong as murder; such an action on the part of a person is to be considered as a rejection of God's divine plan. The pope added that suicide is also a failure to love one's self and a denial of the instinct to live, yet he called Catholics to understand that, at times, psychological factors can hinder or totally remove one's responsibility for suicide. John Paul upheld the belief that one must distinguish between suicide and sacrificing one's life for another. Among the things for which a Christian may sacrifice his or her life, the pope noted 1) in the charitable service of one's fellow humans, 2) to give glory to God, and 3) for the salvation of others. (See also Death/Dying, Morality.)

SYNOD OF BISHOPS   is a meeting of Catholic bishops —with representatives attending from around the world—regularly convened by the pope to discuss important church matters. The synod of bishops is expected to advise the Holy Father about how best to handle the important matters being considered. The term synod comes from the Latin *synodus*, which means "a general meeting."

Larger and more crucial gatherings of church leaders are called councils whereas smaller, limited-in-scope meetings of bishops are called synods. Synodal meetings were held as early as 170 A.D. By the third century such gatherings were being held in many parts of the Christian world. The Council of Nicaea (325 A.D.) set down rules and guidelines for synod meetings. In the 16th century the Council of Trent came up with additional rules that required regular, even yearly, synodal sessions. Quite recently, on September 15, 1965, Pope Paul VI permanently established the current synod of bishops for the universal church. The document in which Paul VI made this announcement was *Apostolica Sollicitudo.*

Vatican Council II declared that it is vitally important for bishops to work together in a collegial way in order to guide and teach the members of the church. The council added that Catholic bishops have the continuing and serious duty to discuss and act upon the pressing problems and issues that affect church life.

The pope as the Bishop of Rome and chief leader and pastor of the church is the president of the official synod of bishops. All meetings of the synod are held under his authority. The synod is asked to advise the Holy Father on important matters by providing information, opinions, and research that will help him to effectively lead, serve, and govern the Catholic Church. Catholics are urged to accept the teachings and statements the pope issues once he has received suggestions and information from the synod of bishops. Six synods have been held from 1967 to the present. Church law now requires the convening of general meetings of the synod every three years.

Note of Interest: Another type of synod held in the church is the diocesan synod, a meeting of selected clergy, religious, and laity, which is called by the local bishop of a Catholic diocese. During diocesan synods participants consider the needs of their local church and advise their bishop on ways to best meet these needs. The bishop is then free to act or not to act on the synod's suggestions. Church law states that each diocese should have a synod every ten years. (See also Bishop, Collegiality, Magisterium.)

SYNOPTICS is a term commonly used for the gospels of Mark, Matthew, and Luke. These books are called "synoptic" because when the texts are laid side by side and "seen at a glance" (synoptic), it becomes evident that they include and report many of the same sayings and events in the life of Jesus Christ. Mark's gospel was written about 65 A.D. in the city of Rome. Both Matthew and Luke wrote their gospels after the year 75 using Mark's work as a source, but not the only source. (See also Luke, Mark, Matthew.)

TABERNACLE is a container in which the Blessed Sacrament (the eucharist) is reserved for adoration and for taking communion to the sick. By keeping the Blessed Sacrament in tabernacles, Catholics acknowledge the continuing presence of Jesus Christ. They sometimes make private visits to church to pray to Jesus in front of the tabernacle.

The tabernacle was used by the Hebrew people during Old Testament time to symbolize God's holy yet invisible presence in their midst. In fact, Yahweh provided details (to the great leader Moses) on how to build and decorate the earliest of tabernacles. (Ex 25-27). In the early church, Christians did not use tabernacles. Rather the eucharist was taken to private homes to keep it safe. In later years the container that held the Blessed Sacrament in churches was placed near the main altar or in some instances was hung above the altar. It had been the custom since the early 1600s to place the tabernacle on the main altar of the church. In 1964 a church instruction stated that tabernacles should be located in places other than the main altar of the church.

Tabernacles can be round, rectangular, or square; their interiors must be made of materials that are fireproof and burglar-proof. Tabernacles may be decorated with precious metals, wood, jewels, and stone.

Catholics are encouraged to make frequent visits to the Blessed Sacrament in order to pray to the Lord. Blessed candles burn at all times near tabernacles that hold the eucharist. (See also Eucharist.)

THEOLOGY   is an ordered attempt to bring to intellectual and insightful formal expression the human experience of faith in God. For centuries theology has been defined (in Saint Anselm's words), as "faith seeking understanding." The living and personal trust in God to which human beings freely assent is interpreted and expressed through theology. The term theology stems from the Latin *theologia*, "knowledge of God."

Christian theology originated with the apostles of Jesus, whose personal witness and catechetical reflections were faith-filled expressions of hope in the Lord. Saint Augustine (a father and doctor of the church), saw theology as reasoning or discourse about God and faith. Saint Thomas Aquinas (13th century), believed that theology was a study of the content of faith to better understand God's revelation. Theology was eventually defined as the rational study of the content of divinely revealed truths and of the specific teachings (doctrines) of the faith of Catholic Christians.

Faith comes from the experience of God and assent to him in the midst of human living; but it is also conviction that results in a free, loving, and wholehearted response to the divine. Theology follows upon faith-experience: it is a process of reflection and a bringing to expression a human being's own personal knowledge of and appreciation for God. Theological expressions can be spoken or written in traditional ways, but can also be expressed in poetic forms: music, dance, and stories.

Theologians are scholars, thinkers, and/or writers who reflect upon and express 1) the meaning of church doctrines, 2) the real experiences of faithful Christians living out the doctrines, norms, and practices of the church community. Theologians have the right and duty to clarify how the Spirit of God is alive and actively present within the people of God. They should also speak out whenever they perceive that a church teaching or norm is erroneous, yet they must always first listen carefully to what the church's magisterium has to say.

In the 20th century church members have benefited from many gifted theologians: Rahner, Congar, Moltmann, Barth, Tillich, Bonhoeffer, Bultmann, Schillebeeckx, Kasper, Macquarrie, Chardin, Gutierrez, Boff, Cone, and many others. There are many branches of theology: dogmatic theology, biblical theology, systematic theology, moral theology, liturgical theology, sacramental theology, historical theology, political theology, liberation theology, existential theology, pastoral theology, process theology, and more.

Praxis is a term that is often used in liberation theology and religious education discussions. *Praxis* involves action and the "practice" of theology that follows reflection and discussion. It leads to additional prayerful, critical reflection on the good news. It is concerned with living faith and the ongoing mission of the people of God. It seeks the renewal and restructuring of society and culture so as t⁻ bring about human rights and liberation for all, authentic social justice, and the dynamic development of the kingdom of God. In religious education a *praxis* approach helps the catechist and students to reflect on effective Christian action, which requires critical reflection on the gospels. In a sense *praxis* in religious education helps link the theory about being a Catholic Christian to real-life, faithful concerns of being a Christ-follower. (See also Faith, Magisterium, Ministry.)

TRADITION is the process by which the Catholic faith is handed on. The church's tradition includes the doctrines (teachings), documents and teachings of church fathers and other leaders, the worship of believers, and the living and active faith of all church members through the ages. There is another kind of tradition—those customs, values, practices, rules, attitudes—that are uniquely Catholic. These traditions should not be confused with *the* tradition of the church. The term tradition is based on the Latin *traditio*, which means "handing down" and "giving over."

The apostles were the first catechists of the Christian community. They handed on all that had been revealed to them by Jesus, his Spirit, and Hebrew scriptures. Through the centuries the church came to believe 1) that divine revelation had ceased at the close of the apostolic age (with the death of the last apostle) and 2) that which had been revealed must be preserved by Catholics and faithfully handed on to generations to come. The Protestant reformers deemphasized the significance of tradition, and centered on scripture as the ultimate source of God's revelation. In fact, their motto was "sola scriptura"—by scripture only. In response, the Council of Trent (1545-1563) maintained that there are two sources of divine revelation: scripture and tradition. Vatican Council II refined this teaching through the statement that there is only one divine source of revelation (a divine wellspring), but *two forms* (which compose one deposit of Catholic faith). These forms are scripture and sacred tradition.

While showing great honor to church tradition, we can say that in a sense revelation is going on even now—as the faith of church members deepens and matures, the purpose and the meanings of that which is revealed become better understood. The church always attempts to express the teachings and truths of the Catholic faith in words and ways that can be better understood and accepted by humankind.

The church teaches that scripture and tradition form an essential unity. Scripture is the inspired Word of God, while tradition is the process by which the church hands on the faith of Catholics. According to Vatican II, the church must preserve, proclaim, and spread the good news of salvation in Christ—giving scripture and tradition equal honor. The council said too that scripture, tradition and the teaching authority of the church (magisterium) are closely bound together, so bound that one cannot stand without the others. (See also Doctrine, Magisterium, Revelation.)

TRENT, COUNCIL OF was the 19th ecumenical council of the church. It was held from 1545 to 1563. Three successive popes, Paul III, Julius III, and Pius IV, presided over this important council. Trent was convened to respond to the Protestant Reformation begun several decades earlier. The Council of Trent attempted to clarify basic teachings of the Catholic faith and to begin a complete reform of the church itself.

This council got underway in Trent, Italy, on December 13, 1545. Church leaders had tried, quite unsuccessfully, for 25 years prior to this date to have Catholic bishops gather for an official council meeting. Only 30 or so bishops were present when Trent began but by the time the council was concluded on December 4, 1563, more Catholic Church leaders had participated. Over 25 major sessions were held during the course of this important council.

Trent ranks as one of the greatest of ecumenical councils, maybe only second to Vatican Council II, for clarifying church teachings and setting disciplines for church members to follow. Trent's response (or counter) to the Protestant reform brought on a new era of Catholic history called the "Counter-Reformation." Unfortunately, it also led the church into a long period of anti-Protestantism, which seriously delayed the process of Christian unity.

The Council of Trent clearly defined a number of significant doctrines of the faith. Trent noted that the bible and tradition are the two, true sources of Catholic teachings. It restated and emphasized church teachings on the eucharist, and formally stated the exact meaning and number of the sacraments. Trent held that salvation is a gift from God; it proposed rules for valid marriages, helped begin seminaries for the formation of men who want to be priests, and it even began an index of condemned books. (This index no longer exists.) (See also Council, Ecumenical; Sacrament; Tradition.)

TRINITY is the dogma of the church which maintains that God is one divine nature yet three divine persons: the Father, the Son, and the Holy Spirit. This is a great mystery, one that human beings do not fully comprehend, but nevertheless one that all believers should accept with deep faith. The church understands that the three persons of God are eternal, equal, yet somehow distinct, and deserve equal reverence and honor from humanity.

An early theology of God can be found in Paul's writings (2 Cor 13:13). Jesus himself adhered to a basic understanding of the Holy Trinity as Father, Son, and Spirit. The Christian belief in God, as divine nature (one substance) in three Persons, was formally expressed in the Nicene Creed and by the Council of Alexandria (both dating from the latter half of the 4th century). The Council of Nicaea (325) explained that Jesus, the truly divine and human son of God, was begotten by the Father. A later provincial council of churchmen, who met in Rome in 385, defined the one God as three equal, eternal distinct persons. Great church thinkers like Augustine, Anselm, and Thomas Aquinas have written and taught about the Holy Trinity. Many major councils of the church have provided teachings on the Trinity—these councils include the Fourth Lateran (1215), Second Lyons (1274), Florence (1438–45), Trent (1545–63), Vatican I (1869–70), and Vatican II (1962–65).

The abiding mystery of the Trinity is impossible to fully explain, yet it is a matter of faith and church tradition. In following Vatican II's reflections on the Trinity as divine loving community, some theologians see a parallel to the Trinity in the unity of all men and women and in love, concern, mercy, justice, and compassion that every person should offer to others. Much speculation on the meaning of the Trinity and on our relationship to God has been done in recent decades. One particular view of God that has emerged says that God is transcendent, beyond, yet still somehow present to and within human beings. Through the Incarnation of the Second Person and the gift of his Spirit to the world, God is present in history. Through his grace humans can enjoy an open, ongoing, ever-deepening relationship with him. Though God is present to them, men and women remain free: God's grace does not deny human creatures the basic freedom to choose the good nor to choose evil. At best humankind can describe what God is like by using human characteristics (loving, caring, faithful, merciful, forgiving, full of compassion, joyful, humorous). Jesus spoke of God as Father (using Abba, "Dad") with the kind of love a child shows in addressing a parent.

The Catholic Church, through Vatican II, has re-emphasized belief that God is the true creator and source of unity for the church and all of humanity. The church is a sacramental sign of the one God in the world and a community of God's people which cares for the many needs of the human race. God existed before time began, has created all that is. As Father he has begotten the Son (his eternal Word) and this Son has reconciled the world to God. The Spirit—the creative love shared by Father and Son—is sent to guide the people of God. A favorite traditional prayer of Catholics is the "Glory Be," which honors the eternal Trinity. The feast of the Holy Trinity—which has ancient roots— is celebrated by the church on the Sunday after Pentecost each year. (See also Christology, Community, Monotheism.)

UNITED STATES CATHOLIC CONFERENCE (USCC) is the secretariat and an agency of the National Conference of Catholic Bishops (NCCB), a civil corporation which carries out much of the civil and religious work of the church in the United States. The USCC is controlled by this body of bishops but it differs from the NCCB in its specific functions and purpose.

The USCC has origins in the National Catholic War Council of 1917 and the National Catholic Welfare Council (founded September 24, 1919), and the National Catholic Welfare Conference Inc., which was a service agency of the bishops of this country. The present USCC assumed the operations of this conference on January 1, 1967.

The chief officers of the USCC are bishops (president, vice-president, treasurer, and general secretary), but it employs other clergy, religious, and lay men and women. The USCC maintains an executive committee; a committee on research, plans and programs; a committee on budget and finance; and a committee on personnel and administrative services. The major departments of the USCC include: Communication, Education (which, until 1982, housed the National Conference of Diocesan Directors of Religious Education (NCDD), and the now defunct National Federation of Catholic Youth Organizations (NCYOF), a youth ministry agency), social development and world peace. Each department is watched over by a committee made up of bishops, priests, and in some cases religious and laypersons. Other USCC offices include general counsel, government liaison, research and planning, and finance and administration.

The Official Catholic Directory notes that the USCC provides the structure and resources needed to insure coordination, cooperation, and assistance in the public, educational and social concerns of the church in the United States, on national and interdiocesan levels. An advisory board—composed of bishops, priests, religious, and laity—continues to offer advice to the USCC on its plans, programs, and endeavors. (See also Bishops, Confraternity of Christian Doctrine, Youth Ministry.)

VATICAN   also known as Vatican City, is a cluster of buildings and shrines inside the city of Rome in which the pope's residence—the papal palace—and St. Peter's Basilica are located. The official name of the Vatican is "Stato della Citta del Vaticano," and it is viewed as a sovereign state. Vatican City has its own post office, radio station, offices for government bureaus, and even a number of fine arts galleries.

The first papal residence was built on the present site of the Vatican by Pope Symmacus in the year 500. The church now known as St. Peter's Basilica was constructed over many years during the 16th and 17th centuries and is the world's largest Catholic church building. For centuries various popes acquired land around the papal residence and St. Peter's. In 1929 the Vatican was officially named the territorial see of the pope of the Catholic Church by the Lateran Treaty; it now measures 110 acres within the city of Rome.

In modern times the Vatican has had diplomatic ties with many other nations of the world. It remains a politically neutral state to this day, its worldly power being much more limited now than in some ages past. The population of the Vatican is approximately 1000, including priests, religious, and a number of laypersons.

The government and authority for running Vatican City rests with the pope but much of the actual work is done by a special pontifical commission. The parish church of the Vatican is St. Ann Church. Of particular note is the Vatican Library which was built by Popes Sixtus IV and V. It maintains over 750,000 books and some 70,000 important and rare manuscripts. (See also Peter, Pope.)

VATICAN COUNCIL I was the 20th ecumenical council of the Catholic Church. In 1864 Pius IX announced that this council would be held in Rome, but it did not get underway until five years later. Vatican I is perhaps best remembered as the council which formally defined the doctrines on the pope's primacy and infallibility.

Vatican I began on December 8, 1869 and took place in St. Peter's Basilica (in the Vatican). About 750 bishops of the church attended. Eighty-nine general sessions and four public sessions were held and the council produced two major documents (called constitutions), *Dei Filius* and *Pastor Aeternus*. Both were published in 1870. The council was concluded on October 20th, 1870.

Vatican I's statements on papal primacy and infallibility are still discussed today. In fact the doctrine of infallibility has been hotly debated in recent years. The church recognizes that its statements on infallibility have sometimes led to debate among modern thinkers but it nevertheless maintains that this official teaching is authentic.

Vatican I also produced significant statements about reason, faith, and divine revelation, and about the evils of several heretical teachings including "pantheism" and "deism." (See also Council, Ecumenical; Infallibility.)

VATICAN COUNCIL II was the 21st and most recent ecumenical council of the church. Vatican II was called for by Pope John XXIII in 1959, but it did not begin until 1962. This council was held in Rome (at the Vatican) with some 2800 church leaders plus other Catholics and non-Catholic persons attending. A total of sixteen major documents was produced by this pastoral council on church renewal including forward-thinking statements on the church itself and the church's liturgy, on divine revelation, the ecumenical movement, Christian education, and the roles of clergy, religious, and laity in church and modern-life.

Pope John led the first of Vatican II's four major sessions. Paul VI led the next three sessions. (John XXIII died in 1963.) Vatican Council II was concluded on December 8, 1965. It has been hailed frequently as one of the most important meetings in the entire history of the Catholic Church.

Pope John hoped that Vatican II, like a new Pentecost, would encourage a great spirit of renewal and enthusiasm among Catholics around the globe. John also wanted the council to provide a much-needed sense of hope-filled expectation to contemporary church members and to bring all Christians closer together through ecumenical unity. Non-voting theologians, religious, laypersons, and even members and representatives of non-Catholic religions were of much assistance to the church fathers during Vatican Council II.

Vatican II was a good example of true collegiality at work among the leaders of the church. The pope and other bishops of the Catholic faith came together as concerned pastors and shepherds in order to teach, direct, and guide the entire Catholic Church. The sixteen documents of this council are some of the finest and most significant writings in recent church history. (See also Collegiality; Council, Ecumenical; John XXIII.)

VESTIBULE   is an anteroom through which Catholics pass in order to reach the main section of a church. One usually enters a vestibule by walking through the main church doors.

Vestibules are like the courtyards that were located near the entrances to homes, palaces, and official buildings in days gone by. Modern church vestibules are sometimes areas in which displays of books and pamphlets, parish announcement boards and church bulletins may be found. Sometimes holy water containers and dispensers are kept near or within church vestibules.

In recent years it has become quite common for the priest who is beginning a Mass to walk in procession from the vestibule area up to the main altar of the church. Often he will return to the vestibule area when the Mass has ended in order to greet those who have attended the eucharistic celebration.

VIGIL LIGHTS   also called votive candles, are wax candles which are lighted by Catholics during prayerful acts of devotion. Vigil lights may be found in a number of places within church buildings. Most often they are located in front of statues of Mary, the saints, and other holy images.

Vigil lights are symbols of deep hope that prayers will be answered and special needs will be filled. A church tradition holds that these lighted candles are symbols of a desire to be with Christ continually, and are lighted in order to keep watch with him in times of trouble and in times when the faithful cannot be present in church.

Vigil lights are Catholic sacramentals. They are usually grouped together in decorative arrangements in a number of places throughout the church building. It is customary that persons lighting these candles leave a small donation to help support the church and to cover the cost of the vigil lights. (See also Candles, Sacramentals.)

VIRTUE   is a spirtual habit, capacity, or quality that helps people to do what is morally good, to avoid evil, and to live as good Christians. The word virtue comes from the Latin *virtus*, to have strength.

The theological virtues are: faith, hope and charity (love). These are given to persons at the time of baptism. The four cardinal virtues, also known as the moral virtues, are: prudence, temperance, justice, and fortitude.

The virtues provide the power(s) to recognize the good and to do good at all times, despite obstacles that could get in the way. They are spiritual gifts and powers, originating in God's divine power and his grace, which grow stronger as they are used and developed. In a sense, they are living ways by which Christians witness that God's grace is living and active in them.

Note of Interest: Asceticism is a way of living, a form of self-discipline important for authentic Christian living, that takes the gospel and the Christian call seriously that we be perfect. True asceticism leads to humble service and love for others, growth in patience, self-acceptance, and commitment to the good news of Jesus and to the building of the kingdom. Those who embrace an ascetic way of life must practice radical self-denial and be totally commited to the Lord. Therefore it involves temperance (moderation in one's desires and behavior. (See also Charity, Faith, Holiness, Hope.)

VOWS   are sacred promises to carry out special actions or lead a way of life centered on dedication to God, imitation of Jesus Christ, and loving and serving the people of God. The word vows comes from the Latin *vovere*, "to promise." Some priests, religious, and modern laypersons live the three vows known as the "evangelical counsels": poverty, chastity, and obedience.

Vows must be made with sufficient knowledge and in freedom. Traditionally Catholic Christians have made different types of vows: *private vows* (those professed without recognition from the offical church), *public vows*, which are ackowledged by the church community, and which are either professed perpetually (for all time) or for specific periods. Persons make vows in an attempt to be more Christlike and better able to serve others. In most cases the vows-for-life that believers have professed are accepted by the church in the midst of a group (an assembled community) of Catholics.

The Second Vatican Council taught that vows are rooted in the ministry, example, and teaching of Jesus—particularly in his love for God and humanity, and in his desire to know the Father's will. Vows are gifts from God, ideals recommended by the great fathers and doctors of the church. Vows are acts of worship and genuine commitments to serve God and others. Vatican II noted that the evangelical counsels of poverty, chastity, and obedience are to be faithfully observed by all religious, including priests within religious orders. (See also Religious Orders.)

WAY OF THE CROSS   is a devotion and a sacramental of the Catholic Church. It is sometimes called the Stations of the Cross. These stations are usually hung on the interior walls of churches and are fourteen illustrations of events of the passion, death, and burial of Jesus. Praying the Way of the Cross helps Catholics to contemplate the salvation offered by God and to gain indulgences when certain conditions are met.

The stations probably got their start from the visits pilgrims made to the Holy Land to view scenes of Jesus' suffering and crucifixion in Jerusalem. The formal devotion now known as the Stations evolved over many centuries—particularly along with a very active devotion to Christ's Passion in the 12th and 13th century church. By the 14th century the Franciscan Order was promoting the stations energetically. Saint Leonard of Port Maurice, for example, preached frequently on the devotion during the 1700s. In 1731 Pope Clement XII established guidelines for the Way of the Cross.

Catholics can pray the stations alone, or in a group with a leader. When alone, they walk from station-to-station and meditate and pray in front of each station. In recent years a 15th station, the resurrection, has been added.

The Stations of the Cross are: 1) Jesus is condemned to death on the cross; 2) Jesus accepts his cross; 3) Jesus falls for the first time; 4) Jesus meets his sorrowful mother; 5) Simon of Cyrene helps Jesus carry his cross; 6) Veronica wipes the face of Jesus; 7) Jesus falls the second time; 8) Jesus speaks to the women of Jerusalem; 9) Jesus falls the third time; 10) Jesus is stripped of his garments; 11) Jesus is nailed to the cross; 12) Jesus dies on the cross; 13) Jesus is taken down from the cross; 14) Jesus is placed in the tomb; 15) (optional) Jesus rises from the dead. (See also Indulgences, Prayer, Sacramentals.)

WITNESS is the Christian example every person initiated into the church (through the sacrament of baptism), is called to give. It is a personal testimony to one's commitment to Christ and the Christian way of life, as well as a sign of a personal desire to seek first the kingdom of God.

Jesus was God's most perfect self-communication, his greatest revelation and finest witness. The apostles were the prime witnesses to the Christ—having experienced the risen Jesus and having been charged by him with spreading the good news of salvation to the whole world. Those Christians who followed the apostles in time continued this crucial mission, and the present members of the church continue to carry on the work of actively witnessing to belief in Jesus and serving people under the guidance of his Spirit.

Personal witness by the baptized can take many forms: good example and works of charity and mercy, moral actions, moral attitudes, true hopefulness, living the Christian life through celebration of the sacraments, worship, and prayerfulness, holiness, genuine humility, participation in the church's ministries, and being active in social justice causes.

Vatican Council II emphasized that the church is a community that bears witness to Christ and a humble people of service whose members strive to imitate the Lord. The council also stressed that baptized persons have a duty, as individual members of the body of Christ, to be living witnesses and examples to those who wish to know more about the kingdom and the eternal, transforming hope which Christians profess. Just as baptism initiates one's responsibility to witness, the sacraments of confirmation and eucharist renew and strengthen the desire to give testimony to faith and loving discipleship.

Note of Interest: Vatican II's *Decree on Ecumenism* urged all Christians to give witness to the reality of common guilt for the divisions which exist in Christianity to this day. The council looked to full, ecumenical unity which will give witness to universal Christian hope and the crying need for justice in the world now. (See also Baptism, Evangelization, People of God.)

WORKS OF MERCY are human actions that are impelled by love of God and other human beings. The mercy which a Christian offers to others is a living sign of the limitless mercy, love, and goodness which the creator has shown and continues to show to all human beings. The church has traditionally spoken of corporal and spiritual works of mercy.

The traditional corporal works of mercy relate to bodily

needs, whereas the spiritual works relate more to the needs of the human soul. Centered in the minstry and perfect example of Jesus, the ability to be merciful is a gift from God that enriches the lives of faithful Christians. Many of the traditional works of mercy, as named by the church, can be traced to Jesus' last judgment discourse (Mt 25:31-46), and to the spirit of Beatitudes (Mt 5:3-10).

Vatican Council II taught that doing the works of mercy affords the most striking testimony of the Christian life in action. The *National Catechetical Directory: Sharing the Light of Faith* reminds Christians that works of mercy and charity are always incumbent upon the church and its members. Some Catholic Christians perform merciful deeds in pastoral care ministries, hospitals, homes for the aged, children's homes, drug-alcohol treatment centers, social service and recreation program centers, and through Catholic Charities' organizations. Missionaries proclaim the gospel message and offer varied forms of relief services to the needy. Catholic Relief Services is one major church agency that assists underpriveleged citizens throughout the world.

The works of mercy are: (Corporal Works) 1) to feed the hungry; 2) to give drink to the thirsty; 3) to clothe the naked; 4) to visit the imprisoned; 5) to shelter the homeless; 6) to visit the sick; 7) to bury the dead. (Spiritual Works) 1) to admonish the sinner 2) to instruct the ignorant; 3) to counsel the doubtful; 4) to comfort the sorrowful 5) to bear wrongs patiently; 6) to forgive all injuries; 7) to pray for the living and the dead. Human mercy is more than compassion only. It is compassion-in-practice extended to those in need, a living testimony to the dignity of human beings. (See also Missions, Social Justice, Witness.)

WORSHIP is prayerful honor and recognition that God (the perfect Other, the Divine, the Holy, the Absolute One) has created all that is. Through worship human beings seek to repond to and be in union with him. The worship of Catholic Christians expresses the belief that Jesus Christ has redeemed the world through his death and resurrection, and that through his church he continues to offer God's grace and salvation to all men and women. The word worship comes from the Old English *weorthscipe*, "to show reverence, honor, dignity."

Both religion and worship (by an individual or by a community of believers) are genuine expressions of what it means for humanity to be creatures dependent upon the loving creator. Prayer-filled worship can be private or public. Saint Augustine emphasized that all worship expressed in communal liturgy should originate in the religious worship of God in one's deepest interior and soul, the heart. Through worship men and women celebrate God's nearness through creation, recognize that they have been redeemed, and ask for God's help in their ongoing struggle for eternal salvation. The good news of the New Testament reveals that Jesus has promised that whenever two or more are gathered in his name—in community—he is really present in their midst (Mt 18:20). The seven sacraments celebrate this continuing, saving presence in a unique way. As prayerful and symbolic actions of God's people, the sacraments express humanity's acceptance that God has mastery and authority over all and that individuals need to express this acceptance and respond to God within a community of believers. Reforms of the liturgy and worship of the church are not meant to do away with the liturgical forms of the past but to revise and improve them so that the entire worshipping community will be able to express—through symbol, prayer, actions, self-sacrifice—their proper relationship with the divine.

The greatest-ever act of worship was Jesus Christ's total giving of himself to God the Father. The finest act of worship by Jesus' community of followers is the eucharist (the Mass). The church recognizes, of course, that many other public and private acts constitute true worship. In the sacraments (especially the eucharist, which Vatican II called a foretaste of the heavenly liturgy), believers honor and celebrate God's gift of grace, and express their belief that God is present with his people offering them full, abundant, everlasting life. (See also Community, Eucharist, Prayer.)

YAHWEH   is the proper name by which the Lord God of Israel was known. When written correctly, using the English alphabet, it is spelled *YHWH*. In English it is pronounced Yahway. The word is sometimes translated "Jehovah," but this is not a correct translation from the original Hebrew. Catholics hold that Yahweh is the same creating, powerful, loving, one God in whom they have faith and hope.

The book of Exodus in the bible says that the name Yahweh was revealed to Moses from a "burning bush." A popular translation of this holy name is, *I am who am*. The specific Hebrew pronunciation of the name Yahweh has actually been lost because the Hebrew people neither spoke nor wrote God's name (out of fear and awe). It was enough for them to understand that they were Yahweh's chosen people, that he was the Lord with whom they had made a loving covenant (Ex 3:14), the God who had led them out of slavery in Egypt and given them the Promised Land.

Though the debate goes on (over how "Yahweh" is to be translated most properly), scripture scholars seem to agree that it is connected with the Hebrew *hawah*, "to be." It has also been proposed that the name could mean "I am who will be" or "He who brings into being whatever comes into being." In any case Yahweh was a Lord active and present among his people wherever he was known, whenever he was called upon.

Yahweh was often thought of in anthropomorphic terms. He was accorded very human characteristics by the Hebrews. As the Lord he was honored as a law-giving God (the chosen people believed that the law of Moses had come down to them directly from Yahweh through the leader Moses). The people remembered the events that had occured thanks to Yahweh: the passover from Egypt, the covenant established at Sinai (plus Yahweh's important words, "I will be your god, and you will be my people"). Yahweh was a protector and guide, a saving God, who helped his people through sufferings in Egypt, starvation during their desert wanderings, and conflicts with many enemies. Yahweh was the God who freely chose to make a self-communication (to reveal himself) in history to great Hebrew leaders and to make great demands on Israel's prophets. Yahweh was a loving and mighty Other in whom the Hebrews had faith. They believed him to be present in a unique way. The Hebrews found identity—social, religious, political, and as individuals—in this caring, revealing God. (See also Covenant, Hebrews, Monotheism.)

YOUTH MINISTRY   is a ministry in the church community which responds to modern youth's particular needs and challenges them to be committed followers of Jesus. Youth Ministry fosters the personal and spiritual growth of young persons, attempts to serve them humbly and to draw them deeply into the heart of the mission and ministry of the people of God.

In 1930 Bishop Bernard J. Sheil initiated a youth program in Chicago, and thus began a dynamic movement (later to be called the CYO) that would stretch from shore to shore in the United States. In the 1940s a national youth organization was founded under the title National Council of Catholic Youth. During the 1950s and 1960s, work among Catholic youth continued to grow and develop, and in the early 1960s many dioceses accepted a recommendation that their youth office be named *Catholic Youth Orgainzation* (CYO). CYO programs tended to be parish-based while offering religious, cultural, social, and athletic activities to draw young people closer to their home parishes. Eventually the headquarters of the National Catholic Youth Organization Federation (NCYOF) were located at the United States Catholic Conference in Washington, D.C.

In the first half of the 1970s "youth ministry" became a more recognized and accepted term among Catholic youth workers (Youth ministry has a rich heritage in many Protestant denominations.). Leaders in the field called for a unified vision of a total ministry to young people. Some adults in parishes began to be designated youth ministers and some dioceses founded Offices of Youth Ministry. In 1976, through the USCC, the document *A Vision of Youth Ministry* listed the philosophy, principles, goals, dimensions, components, and the hope for youth ministry in this country. In 1982, after the NCYOF was severed from the USCC, a new and independent National Federation of Catholic Youth Ministry (NFCYM) was established, with headquarters in Washington, D.C.

Though taking many shapes and creative forms, a parish community's youth ministry can involve as many as seven essential components: ministry of word (youth evangelization and catechesis); ministry of worship; creating community; guidance and healing; justice and service programs; enablement of adults and youth to minister to young people; and advocacy of youth's particular needs. Youth ministry is *to* youth when a community attempts to really hear and respond to youth's hopes and needs. It is *with* youth whenever adults and youth unite to serve the young people of the community. It is *by* youth when young people themselves take action to serve their peers in some way (peer ministry). And it is *for* youth when concerned members of the faith community speak up and act on behalf of youth-in-need who will not be heard without advocates. The church encourages adults who feel called to active work as youth ministers to reflect upon the good news of Jesus and to act as witnesses to Christ in reaching out to younger persons. They are reminded of the story of Emmaus (Lk 24:13–35) and are called to model their own ministries on Jesus Christ, the risen one who brought God's presence into individuals' lives. Adult youth ministers are urged to develop a sense of mutuality with youth and to be committed to the mission of the church community and to on-going, personal conversion to the Christian way.

ZIONISM   is the Jewish national movement originating in the late 1800s. A major goal of Zionism was the establishment of the State of Israel; this goal was achieved in 1948. In the past two decades, the church has made a number of important statements about Catholic-Jewish relations and has participated in some dialogues and projects with Jewish people.

The term Zionism has its roots in the Zion of old; this Zion (or Sion) was a fortress captured by King David, which eventually became the holy city in Israel called Jerusalem—the center of life for God's chosen people in Old Testament times. For many centuries, after the nation of Israel was conquered, the Jews lived in many countries around the world as a dispersed and scattered people. Yet they never lost their deep desire for a return to their homeland in the Middle East. The modern Zionist movement began to seek a new Zion, a permanent state of Israel. This idea was first formally proposed at the First Zionist Congress (held in Switzerland in 1897), and with long-standing assistance from the British and later the United Nations, the current State of Israel was declared on May 14, 1948. In 1952 the 23rd Zionist Congress defined Zionism's tasks as heightening national unity, strengthening the Israeli State, and welcoming Jews from around the world who wish to settle in the ancient homeland.

The church issued official statements about Catholic-Jewish relations in the Vatican II document *Declaration On The Relationship of The Church To Non-Christian Religions* (1965). The council noted that there is a special bond between the new people of God (the church) and the people descended from Abraham (the Jews). It said that the beginnings of faith for Christians can be traced to the patriarchs and prophets of the Hebrew people. The church teaches that it awaits the day when all people, including the Jewish community, will address God with a single voice and seek to do his will.

Catholics are urged to strictly avoid all forms of anti-Semitism (discrimination, hatred, persecution, harrassment) directed at Jewish people. The church clearly declares that the Jewish people of today and of centuries past are in no way cursed nor to blame for the suffering and death of Jesus. The Catholic bishops of the United States set up a secretariat for Catholic-Jewish relations in Washington D.C. in 1967, which works for greater understanding and cooperation among Catholics and Jews. A Vatican commission for religious relations with Jewish people was begun in 1975. Also in 1975, the American bishops urged Catholics to study Chapters 9 and 11 of Paul's epistle to the Romans in order to help them understand the Jewish people's relationship with God, plus their spiritual bond to the new law of Jesus Christ and to their cherished homeland.

Common Prayer, Devotions, and Practices

The Lord's Prayer   Our Father, who art in heaven hallowed be thy name: thy kingdom come; thy will be done on earth as it is in heaven. Give us this day our daily bread; and forgive us our trespasses as we forgive those who trespass against us; and lead us not into temptation, but deliver us from evil. Amen.

Hail Mary   Hail, Mary, full of grace, the Lord is with you! Blessed are you among women, and blessed is the fruit of your womb, Jesus. Holy Mary, Mother of God, pray for us sinners, now and at the hour of our death. Amen.

Glory Be   Glory be to the Father, and to the Son, and to the Holy Spirit: As it was in the beginning, is now, and ever shall be world without end. Amen.

Apostles Creed   I believe in God, the Father almightly, creator of heaven and earth, and in Jesus Christ, his only son, our Lord who was conceived by the Holy Spirit, born of the Virgin Mary, suffered under Pontius Pilate, was crucified, died, and was buried. He descended to the dead. On the third day he rose again. He ascended into heaven, and is seated at the right hand of the Father. He will come again to judge the living and the dead. I believe in the Holy Spirit, the holy catholic church, the communion of saints, the forgiveness of sins, the resurrection of the body, and life everlasting. Amen.

Nicene Creed   We believe in one God, the Father, the Almighty, maker of heaven and earth, of all that is seen and unseen. We believe in one Lord, Jesus Christ, the only Son of God, eternally begotten of the Father, God from God, light from light, true God from true God, begotten, not made, one in being with the Father. Through him all things were made. For us men and for our salvation he came down from heaven: by the power of the Holy Spirit he was born of the Virgin Mary, and became man. For our sake he was crucified under Pontius Pilate; he suffered, died, and was buried. On the third day, he rose again in fulfillment of the scriptures: he ascended into heaven and is seated at the right hand of the Father. He will come again in glory to judge the living and the dead, and his kingdom will have no end. We believe in the Holy Spirit, the Lord, the giver of life, who proceeds from the Father and the Son. With the Father and the Son he is worshipped and glorified. He has spoken through the prophets. We believe in one holy catholic and apostolic church. We acknowledge one baptism for the forgiveness of sins. We look for the resurrection of the dead, and the life of the world to come. Amen.

Sign of the Cross   In the name of the Father, and of the Son, and of the Holy Spirit. Amen.

The Magnificat   My soul proclaims the greatness of the Lord and my spirit exults in God my savior; because he has looked upon his lowly handmaid. Yes, from this day forward all generations will call me blessed, for the Almighty has done great things for me. Holy is his name, and his mercy reaches from age to age for those who fear him. He has shown the power of his arm, he has routed the proud of heart. He has pulled down princes from their thrones and exalted the lowly. The hungry he has filled with good things, the rich he has sent away empty. He has come to the help of Israel his servant, mindful of his mercy—according to the promise he made to our ancestors—of his mercy to Abraham and to his descendants forever. Amen.

Memorare   Remember, O most gracious Virgin Mary, that never was it known that anyone who fled to your protection, implored your help, or sought your intercession, was left unaided. Inspired by this confidence I fly to you, O virgin of virgins, my mother. To you I come, before you I stand, sinful and sorrowful. O mother of the Word Incarnate, despise not my petitions, but in your mercy hear and answer me. Amen.

Come, Holy Spirit   Come, Holy Spirit, fill the hearts of your faithful and kindle in them the fire of your love. Send forth your Spirit, and they shall be re-created; and you will renew the face of the earth. Amen.

A Prayer of Joy and Contrition   O my good God, I thank you for the joys of this day—for the gift of life itself, for family and friends, for all good things which come to me from your creative hand. I am sorry for my daily sins—for selfishness and thoughtlessness, for all that is mean and miserly, for neglect of your many children whom you have called me to love. Direct tomorrow's steps in your path and give me the peace of knowing I am always with you. Amen.

Prayer of Saint Francis   Lord, make me an instrument of your peace: that where there is hatred, I may bring love; that where there is wrong, I may bring the spirit of forgiveness; that where there is discord, I may bring harmony; that where there is error, I may bring truth; that where there is despair, I may bring hope; that where there are shadows, I may bring your light; that where there is sadness, I may bring joy.

Lord, grant that I may seek rather to comfort, than to be comforted; to understand, than to be understood; to love, than to be loved. For it is by giving that one receives; it is by self-forgetting that one finds; it is by forgiving that one is forgiven; it is by dying that one awakens to eternal life. Amen.

Mysteries of the Rosary   Joyful Mysteries: 1) Annunciation, 2) Visitation, 3) Birth of Jesus, 4) Presentation of Jesus in the temple, 5) Finding the Child Jesus in the temple.

Sorrowful Mysteries: 1) Agony in the garden, 2) Scourging at the pillar, 3) Crowning with thorns, 4) Carrying of the cross, 5) Crucifixion.

Glorious Mysteries: 1) Resurrection, 2) Ascension, 3) Descent of the Holy Spirit, 4) Assumption of Mary, 5) Coronation of Mary as Queen of heaven.

Stations of the Cross   1) Jesus Is Condemned to Death; 2) Jesus Accepts His Cross; 3) Jesus Falls the First Time; 4) Jesus Meets His Mother; 5) Simon of Cyrene Helps Jesus to Carry His Cross; 6) Veronica Wipes the Face of Jesus; 7) Jesus Falls the Second Time; 8) Jesus Speaks to the Women; 9) Jesus Falls the Third Time; 10) Jesus Is Stripped of His Garments; 11) Jesus Is Nailed to the Cross; 12) Jesus Dies on the Cross; 13) Jesus Is taken Down From the Cross; 14) Jesus Is Buried; 15) Jesus Is Raised From the Dead.

Commandments of God   1) I, the Lord, am your God; you shall have no other gods besides me. 2) You shall not take the name of the Lord, your God, in vain. 3) Remember to keep holy the sabbath day. 4) Honor your father and your mother. 5) You shall not kill. 6) You shall not commit adultery. 7) You shall not steal. 8) You shall not bear false witness against your neighbor. 9) You shall not covet your neighbor's wife. 10) You shall not covet anything that belongs to your neighbor.

The Great Commandment   You shall love the Lord your God with all your heart, with all your soul, with all your strength, and with all your mind; and your neighbor as yourself.

Jesus' Commandment   Love one another as I have loved you.

The Beatitudes   1) Blessed are the poor in spirit; the reign of God is theirs. 2) Blessed are the sorrowing; they shall be consoled.

3) Blessed are the lowly; they shall inherit the land. 4) Blessed are they who hunger and thirst for holiness; they shall have their fill. 5) Blessed are they who show mercy; mercy shall be theirs. 6) Blessed are the single-hearted; they shall see God. 7) Blessed are the peacemakers; they shall be called sons of God. 8) Blessed are those persecuted for holiness' sake; the reign of God is theirs.

Corporal Works of Mercy   1) Feed the hungry, 2) Give drink to the thirsty, 3) Clothe the naked, 4) Visit the imprisoned, 5)Shelter the homeless, 6) Visit the sick, 7) Bury the dead.

Spiritual Works of Mercy   1) Admonish the sinner, 2) Instruct the ignorant, 3) Counsel the doubtful, 4) Comfort the sorrowful, 5) Bear wrongs patiently, 6) Forgive all injuries, 7) Pray for the living and the dead.

Holy Days of Obligation   Christmas—December 25; Immaculate Conception of Mary—December 8; Solemnity of Mary—January 1; Ascension of our Lord—40 days after Easter; Assumption of Mary—August 15; All Saints Day—November 1.

Days of Fasting and Abstinence   In the United States, all Catholics who have reached age 14 should not eat any kind of meat (must abstain) on Ash Wednesday, Good Friday, and the other Fridays of the lenten season. For Catholics between 21 and 59 years of age, both Ash Wednesday and Good Friday are also fasting days. One full meal and two light meals may be taken on these days.

BIBLIOGRAPHY

The following reference works are suggested for those who wish to study further the topics covered in this book.

Abbott, Walter M., ed. *The Documents of Vatican II*. New York: Guild Press, 1966.

Albright, William F., and David N. Freedman, eds. *The Anchor Bible. Notes and Commentary* (44 vols). New York: Doubleday & Co., 1982.

Bauer, J.B., ed. *Encyclopedia of Biblical Theology*. New York: Crossroad Publishing, 1981.

Carlen, Claudia, I.H.M. *The Papal Encyclicals* (4 vols). Wilmington, NC: McGrath Publishing, 1981.

Dollen, Charles J., *et al.*, eds. *The Catholic Tradition: 2000 Years of Great Writings* (14 vols). Wilmington, NC: McGrath Publishing, 1979.

Foy, Felician, O.F.M., ed. *Catholic Almanac*. Huntington, IN: Our Sunday Visitor Press.

Haring, Bernard, C.Ss.R. *Free and Faithful in Christ: Moral Theology for Clergy and Laity* (2 vols). New York: Seabury Press, 1978.

Harrington, Wilfrid, O.P., and Donald Senior, C.P. *New Testament Message: A Biblical-Theological Commentary* (22 vols). Wilmington, DE: MIchael Glazier, 1980.

Hofinger, Johannes, S.J. *Our Message to Christ*. Notre Dame: Fides/Claretian, 1974.

Know Your Faith (4 vols). Notre Dame, IN: Ave Maria Press.

McBrien, Richard P., S.J. *Catholicism* (2 vols). Minneapolis: Winston Press, 1980.

National Conference of Catholic Bishops. *Sharing the Light of Faith: National Catechetical Directory*. Washington, DC: United States Catholic Conference, 1979.

_____. *Sharing the Light of Faith: An Official Commentary*.

Washington, DC.: United States Catholic Conference, 1981.

New Catholic Encyclopedia (17 vols). New York: McGraw-Hill, 1979.

Official Catholic Directory. New York: P.J. Kenedy & Sons, 1981.

Official Catholic Teachings (6 vols). Wilmington, NC: McGrath Publishing, 1978.

Professional Approaches for Christian Educators (12 vols). Winona, MN: St. Mary's Press.

Rahner, Karl, S.J., ed. *Sacramentum Mundi* (16 vols). New York: Herder and Herder, 1968.

———. Foundations of Christian Faith. New York: Seabury Press, 1978.

Religious Reading: Annotated Bibliography of 6000 Religious Books (4 vols). Wilmington, NC: McGrath Publishing, 1977.

What Are They Saying? (9 vols). Ramsey, NJ: Paulist Press.

Wilhelm, Anthony J. *Christ Among Us* (3rd rev. ed.). Ramsey, NJ: Paulist Press, 1982.

Wintz, Jack., O.F.M., ed. *Catholic Update Series* (4 vols). Cincinnati: St. Anthony Messenger Press.

INDEX OF TERMS

(Those articles below appearing in capital letters indicate a full-length treatment of the subject. The italicized numbers indicate the pages where it is found.)

174

184